# SENIOR AND BOOMERS GUIDE TO HEALTH CARE REFORM AND AVOIDING NURSING HOME POVERTY

*Dennis B. Sullivan Esq, CPA, LLM*
*The Estate Planning and Asset Protection Law Center*

INFINITY
PUBLISHING

Copyright © 2013 by Dennis B. Sullivan Esq, CPA, LLM and the Estate Planning & Asset Protection Law Center

ISBN 978-0-7414-8140-5 Paperback
ISBN 978-0-7414-8141-2 eBook

Printed in the United States of America

Published March 2013

**Portion of Proceeds Will Be Donated to the American Red Cross**

**5% of every copy of the Senior & Boomers Guide to Health Care Reform & Avoiding Nursing Home Poverty will be donated to the American Red Cross' Hurricane Sandy Relief Fund.**

American Red Cross

INFINITY PUBLISHING
1094 New DeHaven Street, Suite 100
West Conshohocken, PA 19428-2713
Toll-free (877) BUY BOOK
Local Phone (610) 941-9999
Fax (610) 941-9959
Info@buybooksontheweb.com
www.buybooksontheweb.com

# CONTENTS

# FOREWORD

You have before you a very important book. In fact, if you read only one book on this particular subject over the next 12 months, you have made a very wise choice. I think after you read the final page you'll agree with me.

These are very important times for those facing health care decisions. In the *Senior & Boomers Guide to Health Care Reform & Avoiding Nursing Home Poverty,* Dennis Sullivan & the team of experts at the Estate Planning & Asset Protection Law Center will point out how changes in our health care system make things drastically different than the past. Nowhere is this fact more evident than in the role the Affordable Care Act will play in your health care resolutions.

In my role as creator, developer and producer of *the Choices for Care DVD and Study Guide* program (www.ChoicesforCare.com) which compares and contrasts the various caregiving options available to consumers (nursing home, assisted living, independent living, adult day care and at-home healthcare), I know first-hand the value of becoming educationally prepared for what lies ahead. Dennis Sullivan and the team of professionals at the Estate Planning & Asset Protection Law Center have taken on the task of laying out vitally important information to help you make intelligent decisions. At a time where investment and retirement income for many is stagnating or even dwindling while medical and health care costs continue to increase, failing to plan is as the saying goes "planning to fail."

Of special interest to me is the fact that Dennis and his team have structured this guide with both Seniors and Boomers in mind. The particular demographic is the subject of legendary marketing guru Dan Kennedy's newest book in his long-running successful "No B.S." series appropriately titled: *The No B.S. Guide to Marketing to*

*Leading-Edge Boomers and Seniors.* I'm pleased to be Dan's co-author on this latest book. As a result of my extensive research into the entire Boomers and Seniors demographic for my chapters in this book, I'm acutely aware of the need for enlightened information contained in the guide. That's why I was thrilled to hear about the *Senior & Boomers Guide to Health Care Reform & Avoiding Nursing Home Poverty* and welcomed an advance look at what it offered.

This book is your complete A to Z blueprint for navigating what could easily turn into a minefield of trouble for the less informed. Accordingly, the experts at The Estate Planning and Asset Protection Law Center of Dennis Sullivan & Associates have laid out in easy-to-ready and even easier-to-follow fashion a handy resource and reference manual for anyone interested in coming to terms with and mastering what it takes to successfully comprehend the volatile health care and long term care landscape.

These are very challenging times for Boomers and Seniors of which I'm one of millions in the United States. The health care choices, and the financial wherewithal to deal with these choices, are vastly different than what our parents and grandparents faced. In fact, the entire health care and financial environment has drastically changed in just the past 12-18 months, to where our parents and grandparents wouldn't even recognize it! Therefore, the need for a concise volume such as this one that cuts across the clutter and misinformation dotting the countryside has never been more important.

I first became familiar with Dennis Sullivan several years ago when he invested in my *Choices for Care* program to use to help people and their families. This immediately told me that Mr. Sullivan and the professionals at the Estate Planning & Asset Protection Law Center wanted to give people and their families every opportunity to make good health and long term care decisions. The fact that he and his team have produced the *Senior & Boomers Guide to Health Care Reform & Avoiding Nursing Home Poverty* further emphasizes the ideal that the Estate Planning & Asset Protection Law Center is there to help people just like you to become better prepared for the journey ahead.

Congratulations on making a great decision and receiving this book. That's the first step. Now dive in and prepare to read, review and most of all learn!

With best wishes on your health care journey,


Chip Kessler

# PREFACE

The information in the *Senior and Boomers Guide to Health Care Reform and Avoiding Nursing Home Poverty* has been assembled by our team of caring and dedicated professionals, with seniors and boomers needs in mind. We have developed this helpful guide because so many people are concerned and confused. Investment and retirement accounts have been reduced, although medical and long-term care costs continue to rise.

The stock market has been fluctuating considerably. The values of investment and retirement accounts for seniors have fluctuated as well. Many were relying on these funds to see them through their retirement and senior years. With the economy still sluggish, and recovery slow, determining where money will come from to support a comfortable retirement is a difficult question to answer. Today, many seniors and boomers continue to work long after traditional retirement age.

There is growing concern that many will not be able to enjoy the same quality retirement that previous generations of retirees have enjoyed. The future for many will largely be determined by their ability to keep working and by the availability of government assistance. Today's seniors and boomers find themselves asking questions that were unheard of only a generation ago.

One fact giving rise to these senior and boomer concerns is people are living so much longer than ever before. Since 1900, the average life expectancy of Americans has nearly doubled. For a sixty-five-year-old couple, the odds of one spouse living until age ninety are over 50 percent. As a result of people living longer, they need more money and resources to care for themselves. This fact feeds into another issue of concern for many: our economy and its impact on savings, investments, and taxes.

In addition to personal financial concerns, seniors and boomers are concerned because medical and nursing home costs continue to rise. In our area of Massachusetts, a one month stay in a nursing home can cost as much as $12,000-$15,000. In just one year, the total can balloon to $180,000. Not many people have $180,000 to pay for nursing home care. Many people are surprised to learn that Medicare does not pay for long-term care beyond a brief rehabilitative portion of expenses following hospital care. Unfortunately, many people also find out after it's too late. Medicaid does pay for long-term care, but only after your life savings are reduced to a very low level if preventative steps are not taken. Chapter 9 of this guide will help you discover what you can do to avoid nursing home poverty.

The Affordable Care Act adds confusion to an already difficult and puzzling area. The confusion is centered on what the Affordable Care Act actually does and does not do, and how the changes will be paid for. This guide provides guidance for seniors and boomers on health care reform, as well as how to avoid nursing home poverty. Those eligible for Medicare, as well as individuals in the highest tax brackets, will bear the burden of paying for the Affordable Care Act. See chapter 8 on taxes to pay for the Affordable Care Act.

There are a number of understandable concerns that exist. To help alleviate confusion and provide some guidance, we created *The Senior and Boomers Guide to Health Care Reform and Avoiding Nursing Home Poverty*. You will discover how the Affordable Care Act will impact your family, health care, Medicare coverage, and Medicaid coverage. You will also uncover hidden benefits and steps you can be taking now to avoid nursing home poverty.

The professionals at **The Estate Planning & Asset Protection Law Center of Dennis Sullivan & Associates** help people and their families protect their spouses, homes, life savings and legacies from increasing medical and nursing home costs, taxes, and the costs and time delays of probate. Our unique education and counseling process puts people in charge of their own planning so that they are able to better understand and plan for a protected future.

In an effort to guide patients, the Affordable Care Act provides for "navigators" to help patients through the health care system. The navigator will assist patients as they try to discern their health care options and make the best decision. At the Estate Planning & Asset Protection Law Center of Dennis Sullivan & Associates, we help people and their families concerned with increasing nursing home and long-term care costs. Our unique education and counseling process, which we have been developing and improving for many years, is like a GPS navigation system. Our goal is to put each person and family in charge of their financial and health care decisions for the rest of their lifetime. Under the Affordable Care Act, Medicaid will continue to provide long-term care for those who live in nursing homes, as it has in the past. The new law also strives to broaden the reach of Medicaid beyond nursing home payments, to help those who stay in their own homes and need help living day-to-day. States like Massachusetts, that develop home and community based care models will be offered more federal money for in-home and assisted living care programs.

In Massachusetts, we are ahead of the other states in providing programs to help seniors stay out of nursing homes. As part of our services at the Estate Planning & Asset Protection Law Center, we even help families evaluate both their health care and financial options. We also help people find available state and federal programs and resources to provide for their care. Our professional team includes a registered nurse who has many years of experience in various health care roles; experience with facilities, including hospitals, nursing homes, and assisted living; as well as planning for and transitioning to in-home care. Our professionals have even had success helping families qualify for a number of community care programs including veterans' benefits, MassHealth, Community MassHealth's Frail Elder Program, as well as the Program for All-Inclusive Care for Elders. These are the wave of the future for senior care as people prefer to stay at home or in the community, especially since these options are much less expensive than hospitals or nursing homes.

In our experiences helping people for over twenty-five years, we have found that families who plan ahead and take responsibility for their care have the best protection and the most flexible living and long-term care planning options. In short, those who plan ahead obtain both peace of mind and a better quality of life. Sadly, for many people when they are out of money they are out of options. This, however, does not have to happen to you and your family! We have even been able to help those families who found themselves in an emergency situation, as well as those who have failed to plan ahead, to get the care they need and some help to pay for it without going broke.

The areas where people have questions and concerns often include Medicare, Medicaid, veterans' benefits, financial planning, health care, tax law, long-term care planning, and asset protection planning. We even collaborate with national networks of other experienced professionals so that we are able to monitor changes in the law and uncover new strategies in order to better help people protect what they have and receive benefits that may be available to them now or in the future.

WE HOPE THAT YOU FIND THE
*SENIOR AND BOOMERS GUIDE TO HEALTH CARE REFORM AND AVOIDING NURSING HOME POVERTY* INFORMATIVE AND HELPFUL.

# CHAPTER ONE:
# WHAT ARE SENIORS AND BOOMERS CONCERNED ABOUT?

According to a recent survey of seniors around the country, the following consistently came up as the top concerns:

1. How does health care reform affect seniors?

2. What is the best way to plan ahead and pay for long-term care?

3. Is it possible to pay for a nursing home, or avoid one altogether, without going broke?

Seniors all around the country are concerned about their future, finances, and health care. In short, the stock market, investment accounts, and retirement accounts have fluctuated wildly in recent years, causing many seniors to sell at a loss or keep their savings in their bank accounts, which provides no opportunity for growth. At the same time, costs continue to rise. In the Greater Boston area, one month in a nursing home costs an average of $12,000 to $15,000. Considering these significant concerns, along with the massive changes brought by the new Affordable Care Act, it is understandable why people are so concerned. It is our hope that this guide will provide a continuing resource for you and your family, to help you obtain peace of mind by successful planning for the years to come. Our team of professionals is committed to helping seniors and their families obtain the level of health care they need without going broke paying for it. This guide will address many of the most common questions and concerns of Massachusetts seniors and boomers. The guide will also reveal little known benefits and planning techniques that have already helped hundreds of smart families, not just in Massachusetts but across the country.

Many issues that we need to consider were unheard of a generation ago, and they will continue to affect seniors, boomers, and their families for the foreseeable future. They include:

- Will rising health care costs threaten your economic well-being?

- How will you pay for long-term care, if it is needed?

- How can you leave a financial legacy to your loved ones without paying unnecessary taxes?

- Who do you trust for help in understanding what your options are and what you should do?

At the Estate Planning & Asset Protection Law Center of Dennis Sullivan & Associates, we have created a unique process to help people and their families understand these important topics so they can make informed decisions about their health care and their future. Our unique educational and counseling process puts people in charge of their planning so they are able to understand their current situation as they plan for a protected future. Our team of professionals is dedicated to helping people protect their homes, spouse and life savings from increasing medical and nursing home costs, taxes, and the costs and time delays of probate.

# CHAPTER TWO:
## TODAY'S SENIORS ARE LIVING LONGER

Today's senior is very different from their counterpart of just a decade or two ago. Several factors, including increased longevity, continued employment, and a changing sense of self, have combined to transform the traditional concept of the senior lifestyle. Americans today are living longer than ever before. On average, men and women who reach age sixty-five can expect to live well into their eighties. In fact, the average life expectancy in the United States recently reached an all-time high of 78.7 years, and the Census Bureau estimates that, in the near future, the average life expectancy will be into the low nineties! People must take responsibility for their own successful living and plan ahead for the costs, including medical care needs. Because of increasing longevity, you need to save what you can and protect what you have.

The current trends and realities point to one conclusion: American workers today must assume greater responsibility to ensure they are comfortable long into their golden years. The changing nature of health benefits and increasing costs of medical and long-term care highlight the need for seniors to rely on their own resources and their own savings more than ever before. Today's reality of increasing federal budget deficits and a senior population that is growing five times faster than other segments of the population means that it will be impossible for the government to take care of seniors' health needs to the level it had in the past. There is simply not enough money in the budget to pay for it.

Because these trends will continue to require personal, federal, and state resources, we must all assume greater responsibility to save and plan. Those who successfully save, plan and protect will enjoy greater options and flexibility in their lifestyle, health and long-term care in the years ahead.

© 2013 The Estate Planning & Asset Protection Law Center of Dennis Sullivan & Associates

# CHAPTER THREE:
## LIVING EXPENSES IN RETIREMENT YEARS

While some expenses may disappear—such as commuting to work and paying payroll taxes—other expenses are likely to increase, *including the cost of health care*. As people age, the chance of developing a chronic condition or physical or cognitive disability for which they will require assistance increases significantly. According to one study, 70 percent of all Americans over age sixty-five will require some long-term care services at some point in their lives, while over 40 percent will need care in a nursing home for some period of time. Recent studies also indicate that 50 percent of people over the age of eighty will require some type of skilled care. The World Alzheimer's Organization also reports that 50 percent of people over the age of eighty will have some form of dementia.

Unfortunately, many people mistakenly believe that the state or federal government will pay for all of their long-term care expenses; consequently, they do not do any long-term care planning. Before relying on the government, however, one must consider the following facts:

- It has become increasingly clear **Medicare** only pays for skilled care in a nursing facility for a short period—no longer than and often time less than one hundred days—and only if the patient meets all of Medicare's requirements for receiving daily skilled care. Medicare does *not* cover long-term custodial care or illnesses, such as Parkinson's, Alzheimer's, or dementia.

- **Medicaid** will pay for long term custodial care, but requires individuals to **spend down** most of their savings and income before they are eligible for long-term care benefits. Also, these assets are subject to a current 5 year, but proposed 10 year look-back period on asset transfers and gifts. So people cannot give away assets just to meet eligibility criteria.

Transfers during the look-back period create a penalty period of ineligibility to receive nursing home benefits. Another major problem is that the penalty period does not even begin until the person in the nursing home is out of money! So they are unable to pay for the nursing home during this period of ineligibility. As a result, Medicaid will pay for long-term care expenses only if they become impoverished—that is, they have income and assets below the state's poverty level.

It is important to note, however, that people planning well in advance can prevent nursing home poverty. Please continue reading if you would like to learn more about how people are able to successfully plan ahead for and achieve a protected future.

Today, longer life expectancies and the increasing eventual need for some type of long-term care are making life a lot different for this generation of seniors and for boomers who will eventually become seniors. Today's senior is responsible for ensuring that his or her spouse, home, family, and life savings are protected. At the Estate Planning & Asset Protection Law Center, we are dedicated to helping clients gain the peace of mind of knowing that they will get the care they need without having to sacrifice their hard-earned life savings.

# CHAPTER FOUR:
## HOW THE AFFORDABLE CARE ACT IMPACTS SENIORS

Because of the increasing concerns of so many people, as well as how the new law will drastically affect the lives of us all, we need to understand the Affordable Care Act and how it impacts health care, protection, and planning. There are favorable aspects of the Affordable Care Act, including providing important benefits, such as free preventive services, free annual wellness visits, and a 50 percent discount on prescription drugs for Medicare recipients in the coverage gap known as the "donut hole."

You can also work with your doctor to create a personalized prevention plan. The new health care law will help save money for seniors and ensure people with Medicare can see the doctors they know and trust. The act also creates savings by introducing a number of cuts and reductions in payments to providers, which is explained in the sections that follow.

The new law will not reduce the cost of nursing home care, which can average $12,000 to 15,000 per month. The Affordable Care Act will not pay for Parkinson's, Alzheimer's, or nursing home care. The act will not reduce the burden on a married couple if one spouse needs nursing home care. Spouses are obligated to pay for long-term care costs that can range from $150,000 to $180,000 per year.

# CHAPTER FIVE:
# WHAT KEY FACTORS FOR SENIORS AND BOOMERS ARE PROVIDED FOR IN THE AFFORDABLE CARE ACT?

## I. Closing the Medicare Donut Hole

When a Medicare beneficiary exceeds $2,970 in prescription drug costs for one year, they are in the category known as the donut hole until such time as their drug costs exceed $4,750. Previously, if you were in the donut hole you were responsible for all drug costs. For 2013, however, if you have high prescription drug costs that put you in the donut hole, you now get a 50 percent discount on covered brand-name drugs while you're in the donut hole. The discount will be increased each year until it reaches 75 percent in 2020, when the donut hole is eliminated, enabling Medicare beneficiaries to pay 25 percent of the cost of all their drugs up to the annual out-of-pocket spending limit. Between today and 2020, you'll get continuous Medicare coverage for your prescription drugs. See the next page for a detailed chart. Individuals enrolled in Medicare Part D who have high prescription drug needs will save on their drug costs instead of paying the full cost of their medications once they hit a preset limit, with the donut hole being closed by 2020.

## Standard Part D Plan (as of 2013)

| Prescription Drug Costs | Payments | Costs to Enrollee |
|---|---|---|
| First $325 | Enrollee Pays 100% | $325 |
| $325 to $2,970 | Enrollee Pays 25%; Part D Pays 75% | $661.25 |
| $2,970 to $6,733.75 | Enrollee is in the donut hole and pays 47.5% for brand name drugs and 79% for generic drugs | $3,763.75 |
| | *At this point, total drug costs have reached $6,733.75, and the enrollee has paid $4,750 out of pocket* | |
| Above 6,733.75 | Enrollee pays a nominal amount; Part D picks up 95% | Enrollee pays a nominal co-pay or 5% of costs |

## II. No Co-pays from Medicare Part B

Medicare covers certain preventive services without charging you the Part B coinsurance or deductible. Prior to the Affordable Care Act, Medicare beneficiaries were required to pay a deductable and 20 percent co-pay for preventative services. Under the Affordable Care Act, seniors will also be offered a free annual wellness exam and will not be required to pay for preventative services.

## III. A $716 Billion Savings in Medicare Spending

The life of the Medicare Trust Fund will be extended as a result of savings by reducing waste, fraud and abuse, and slowing cost

8

growth in Medicare. These changes are anticipated to provide seniors and boomers with future cost savings on their premiums and co-insurance.

The act aims to achieve savings in the Medicare program by introducing a series of payment reforms, service delivery innovations, and increased efforts to "reduce waste and abuse."

The Affordable Care Act also aims to improve the way care is delivered to people suffering from chronic diseases. The act creates a new office to coordinate the health and long-term care of people on both Medicare and Medicaid. The act also encourages doctors, hospitals, and nursing homes to work as a team to improve care for people with chronic illnesses. As an example, the act creates a new program that will provide grants to hospitals to encourage coordination of care with community-based providers in an effort to prevent chronic readmission of patients to hospitals.

# CHAPTER SIX:
# HOW WILL MEDICARE SAVINGS BE ACHIEVED?

The Affordable Care Act slows future Medicare spending by reducing overpayments to private insurance plans, restructuring increases in payments to providers, and by tying payment to the quality of care provided. These savings will be achieved through a number of cuts and payment adjustments as described below.

## I. Reducing Payments to Private Insurance Plans

The greatest amount of savings in the Medicare program will be created by reducing overpayments to private Medicare Advantage plans. Before the Affordable Care Act, these private Medicare Advantage plans were paid on average 9 to 13 percent *more* than the average Medicare program to provide the same care. Medicare Advantage overpayments will be phased out by the Affordable Care Act. The act will set payment benchmarks based on each national county, and the Medicare Advantage plans will be paid a fixed percentage of traditional Medicare costs. As a result, plans in rural and suburban areas may continue to see overpayments to Medicare Advantage plans, whereas plans in higher paid counties may see substantial reductions in overpayments.

## II. Reduction in Increases for Payments to Providers

The Affordable Care Act will not reduce payments to providers, but it will reduce the amount that payments will *increase*. Payment updates for providers will be increased based on an update to the "market basket" specific to the provider. These increases will be only by a specific productivity adjustment that reflects the increased cost in doing business for the provider.

10

## III. Changes in Payments to Physicians

Payments to physicians are based on a formula called the sustainable growth rate, which comes from the Balanced Budget Act of 1997. Congress has delayed the application of the formula because it would have resulted in negative updates to payments for physicians. The Affordable Care Act failed to make any updates or revisions to the sustainable growth rate. As a result, the cuts remain a potential threat to access to doctors for Medicare beneficiaries. However, the recent American Taxpayer Relief Act, enacted on New Year's Day, prevents scheduled 27% reimbursement cuts to physicians in 2013.

## IV. Linking Payment to Quality Outcomes

Congress has placed emphasis on efforts to measure quality of care and to provide payment for only those services and procedures that meet certain quality of care standards. The Affordable Care Act is a substantial step in this direction. The act links payment to quality outcomes for health care providers treating Medicare beneficiaries. Under the act, payments to providers may also be reduced to those entities that fail to provide quality care. Payments to a hospital may be reduced if that hospital is determined to have excessive readmissions or procedures that are high in cost and likely to result in readmission to a hospital (the same or different, within a time frame set by the Secretary of Health and Human Services).

## V. Payment Policy Making Shifts to an Independent Advisory Board

The Independent Payment Advisory Board (IPAB) will take over, from Congress, the responsibility of establishing the Medicare payment policies. The board will consist of fifteen full-time members, appointed by Congress and be advised by a ten member consumer advisory council. As a result of the Affordable Care Act's strict guidelines for IPAB action, it is anticipated that the IPAB will be able to achieve additional savings of $15.5 billion from 2014 to 2019. The law prohibits the IPAB from changing eligibility, benefits, or reducing the Part D low-income subsidy. What has

11

many people concerned is that the IAPB, together with the newly formed advisory board, may deny seniors medical care to which they would otherwise be entitled. In-Home and Community Care Resources

## VI. In-Home and Community Care Resources

Home and community-based care programs will be expanded under the Affordable Care Act. As states adopt these programs, seniors will be able to get care and assistance at home as long as they are safely able to remain there. Currently, state Medicaid spending flows primarily to nursing home care. The Affordable Care Act aims to make it possible for seniors to receive long-term care and support services at home and in the community. The act provides incentives to encourage states to shift Medicaid spending from institutions like nursing homes to community-based service providers and resources. In summary, the implementation of these at the state level will be encouraged by the federal government by providing extra federal funds to states with community programs, as provided for in the Affordable Care Act.

Massachusetts is ahead of the rest of the country in developing community-based programs. Therefore it provides a model for community based programs being encouraged in other states. The professionals at the Estate Planning & Asset Protection Law Center of Dennis Sullivan & Associates have had success helping seniors, including those who had emergency situations or little or no prior planning, locate community-based resources for the help they need.

# CHAPTER SEVEN:
# THE BOTTOM LINE

Though the Affordable Care Act offers seniors some significant benefits, the bottom line remains the same. For seniors and those who currently receive Medicare, the Affordable Care Act significantly reduces federal funding of the program over the next decade. Many are wondering who is going to be paying for the Affordable Care Act's ambitious goals. The answer is quite simple, if you receive Medicare assistance, *you* will be paying for the act through the billions in reduced spending. Additionally, if you need nursing home care, your home and life savings could be at risk. In our area of Massachusetts, you may be required to pay $12,000 to $15,000 per month to the nursing home. The annual cost of nursing home care for one person ranges from $150,000 to $180,000. You will also be required to spend down assets to $2,000 for a single person and $113,640 for a married couple. If you take action, you can plan ahead, avoid nursing home poverty, and protect your spouse, home, and life savings from the dangers of increasing medical and nursing home costs. Because the Congressional Budget Office is looking at increasing the look-back from 5 to 10 years, it is critical to take action before additional lengthening of the look-back period takes place.

Needless to say with your future and life savings at risk, it is critical to identify and *eliminate dangers*, review your *opportunities for a protected future*, and *avoid nursing home poverty*. Families can learn more through the helpful guides, reports, and DVDs available at www.DSullivan.com. You can also begin to develop a plan for a protected future by attending a live workshop hosted by our team of professionals. You will gain the confidence and understanding to see your current situation and begin to take the steps that will result in a protected future for you and your family. Call (800) 964-4295 or visit www.DSullivan.com to register to attend an upcoming workshop. If you are not able to attend a live workshop, helpful DVDs are also available.

# CHAPTER EIGHT:
# QUICK SUMMARY OF THE TAXES TO PAY
# FOR HEALTH CARE REFORM

The Affordable Care Act introduced a number of tax changes scheduled for 2013. Here's a quick summary of the major tax provisions that will take effect in 2013:

- The amount that you can contribute to your flexible spending account will be limited to $2,500.

- If you're under age sixty-five, your medical expenses will have to exceed 10 percent (rather than 7.5 percent) of your adjusted gross income to be deductible.

- A new 0.9 percent Medicare tax on wages and self-employment income, above $200,000 on a single return and above $250,000 on a joint return, goes into effect. The Medicare payroll tax is unlimited and is part of the social security tax (FICA) withheld from the employee's checks and matched by employers. The FICA tax is 6.2 percent up to wages/earnings of $110,100 beginning in 2012. The Medicare portion is 1.45 percent on 100 percent of all wages/earnings ad infinitum. Together these two taxes total 7.65 percent. Now, for those with higher incomes, an additional 0.9 percent Medicare tax will be calculated on the individual's 1040 form, but it will not be withheld by employers.

  What no one is talking about is the fact that *this additional 0.9 percent tax will be levied on joint (total) household income*—not just on the individual taxpayer who earns more than $250,000. This means that one spouse could earn $190,000 and the other $65,000 (both of which are under $250,000), but the tax would be imposed on the total above the $250,000 amount allotted on their combined income.

- A new 3.8 percent Medicare tax on net investment income (unearned income) goes into effect for those people with an AGI (adjusted gross income) over $200,000 (single return) or $250,000 (joint return). Investment income includes:

  - dividends

  - interest

  - rental income

  - royalties

  - long-term and short-term capital gains

  - gains on sale of a personal residence above the exclusions of $250,000 (single) or $500,000 (joint)

  - sales of partnership interests or S-corporation stock

  - passive income from partnerships

  - some annuities

This new Medicare tax will also apply to trusts and estates that are already taxed at the highest rates of any—a trust reaches the 35 percent top bracket at just $11,201.

Though future tax legislation could change these provisions, you should be aware of them in your tax planning for this year and next.

Next up, this guide reveals secrets that will enable you to protect your spouse, home, and life savings, while still obtaining the quality long-term care you need.

# CHAPTER NINE:
## HAVE YOU PROTECTED YOUR HOME, SPOUSE AND LIFE-SAVINGS? WHY IS THIS SO IMPORTANT? WHAT CAN YOU DO?

Americans are living longer than ever before. At the turn of the twentieth century, the average life expectancy was about forty-seven years. As we enter the twenty-first century, life expectancy has almost doubled. As a result, we face more challenges and transitions in our lives than ever before. One of the most difficult transitions someone can face is the change from independent living in the person's own home or apartment to living in a long-term care facility or nursing home.

There are many reasons why this transition is so difficult. One is the loss of home—a home where somone lived for many years with a lifetime of memories. Another is the loss of independence. Still another is the loss of the level of privacy enjoyed at home, since nursing home living is often shared with a roommate.

Most people who make the decision to move to a nursing home do so during a time of great stress. Some have been hospitalized after a stroke, some have fallen and broken a hip, and still others have progressive dementia, like Alzheimer's disease or Parkinson's. Whatever the reason, the person can no longer be cared for at home.

The spouse or relative who helps a person transition into a nursing home during a time of stress faces the immediate dilemma of how to find the right nursing home. The task is no small one, and a huge sigh of relief can be heard when the right home is found, and the loved one is moved into the nursing home. For many, the most difficult task is just beginning: How to cope with nursing home bills that may total $12,000 to $15,000 per month or $150,000 to $180,000 per year?

It is also critical to make sure that you (or the person you are trying to help) have all the necessary legal documents in place to authorize someone to make health care and financial decisions in the event that you are unable to make your own decisions. This includes having the right documentation such as:

- Health care proxy and living will or other appropriate advanced directive, which varies from state to state;

- Power of Attorney; and

- HIPAA Authorization

It is also very important that these documents be updated to be sure they reflect your current wishes and to ensure they will be accepted by financial and health care organizations. This is one of the many reasons we created the Lifetime Protection Program to help clients keep documents up to date as well as available when they are needed. We have seen situations when these documents were not available when needed and the spouse and family were not permitted to participate in the health and financial decisions as a result. Rather these families were forced to go to court to seek permission in the courtroom to be able to participate in important and financial decisions on behalf of the incapacitated person. As you can imagine, this is a time consuming and expensive process especially as compared to having your documents up to date and available when needed.

# CHAPTER TEN:
## HOW TO PAY FOR NURSING HOME CARE

One of the things that concerns people most about nursing home care is how to pay for that care. There are basically four ways that you can pay the cost of a nursing home:

1.  **Long-term care insurance:** If you are fortunate enough to have this type of coverage, it may go a long way toward paying the cost of the nursing home. The types of care and services that may be covered by a long-term care insurance policy range from highly skilled nursing care to unskilled custodial care. It might also include care in the home, adult daycare services, assisted living, and respite care. Long-term care insurance has been purchased by some people facing nursing home care, but most people facing a nursing home stay do not have this coverage.

2.  **Pay with your own funds:** This is the method many people are required to use at first. Quite simply, it means paying for the cost of a nursing home out of your own pocket. Unfortunately, with nursing home bills averaging between $12,000 and $15,000 per month in our area, *few people can afford to pay for a long-term stay in a nursing home.*

3.  **Medicare:** This is the national health insurance program primarily for people sixty-five years of age and older, certain younger disabled people, and people with kidney failure. Medicare provides short-term assistance with nursing home and rehabilitation costs, but only if you meet the strict qualification rules, including recovering from an illness or rehabilitating from an injury. If there is no possibility of recovery due to the nature of the illness or injury, Medicare is not available. As we have explained in the previous sections of this guide, the Affordable Care Act has created a

19

number of changes and cuts that will decrease the Medicaid funding available in the future.

4. **Medicaid:** This is a federal and state-funded and administered program that can pay for the cost of the nursing home if certain asset and income tests are met. These income and asset tests are very low, meaning you will be required to spend most of your income and nearly all of your lifesavings to pay for a nursing home, unless you have taken the necessary steps in advance to protect your home and life savings so they will not be used to pay for long term care costs.

## I. What about Medicare?

There is a great deal of confusion about Medicare and Medicaid. Medicare is the federally funded and state administered health insurance program primarily designed for older individuals (i.e., those over age sixty-five). There are some limited long-term care benefits that can be available under Medicare. In general, if you are enrolled in the traditional Medicare plan, you have had a hospital stay of at least three days, and then you are admitted into a skilled nursing facility (often for rehabilitation or skilled nursing care), Medicare may pay for a while. (If you are a Medicare managed care plan beneficiary, a three-day hospital stay may not be required to qualify.)

If you qualify, traditional Medicare may pay the full cost of the nursing home stay for the first twenty days and can continue to pay the cost of the nursing home stay for the next eighty days, but with a deductible that's nearly $120 per day. Some Medicare supplemental insurance policies will pay the cost of that deductible. For Medicare managed care plan enrollees, there is no deductible for days twenty-one through one hundred, as long as the strict qualifying rules continue to be met. So, in the best case scenario, the traditional Medicare or the Medicare managed care plan may pay up to a hundred days for each "spell of illness." In order to qualify for the hundred days of coverage, however, the nursing home resident must be receiving daily skilled care and generally must continue to improve. (Note: Once the Medicare and managed care beneficiary has not received a Medicare-covered level of care for sixty consecutive days, the beneficiary may again be eligible for the hundred days of skilled nursing coverage for the next spell of illness.) While it's never possible to predict at the outset how long Medicare will cover the rehabilitation, from our experience, it usually falls far short of the hundred-day maximum. Even if Medicare does cover the hundred-day period, what then? What happens after the hundred days of coverage have been used? At that point, you're back to one of the other alternatives: long-term care insurance, paying the bills with your own assets, or qualifying for Medicaid.

## II. What Is Medicaid?

Medicaid is a benefits program that is primarily funded by the federal government and administered by each state. In Massachusetts, Medicaid is referred to as MassHealth. Caution: Although Medicaid is a federal program, the rules can vary from state to state. One primary benefit of Medicaid is that, unlike Medicare (which only pays for skilled nursing), the Medicaid program will pay for long-term care in a nursing home once you have qualified. Medicare does not pay for treatment for all diseases or conditions. For example, a long-term custodial stay in a nursing home may be caused by Alzheimer's or Parkinson's disease, and even though the patient receives medical care, the treatment will not be paid for by Medicare. These stays are called custodial nursing stays. Medicare does not pay for custodial nursing home stays. In that instance, you'll either have to pay privately (i.e., use long-term care insurance or your own funds), or you'll have to qualify for Medicaid.

## III. Why Seek Advice for Medicaid and Long Term Care Planning?

As life expectancies and long-term care costs continue to rise, the challenge quickly becomes how to pay for these services. Many people cannot afford to pay $12,000 to $15,000 or more per month for the cost of a nursing home, and those who can pay for a while may find their life savings wiped out in a matter of months, rather than years. Fortunately, the Medicaid program is there to help. In fact, Medicaid has become the long-term care insurance of the middle class, with two thirds of nursing home residents currently receiving government benefits. But the eligibility to receive Medicaid benefits requires that you pass certain tests on the amount of income and assets that you have. Before the Affordable Care Act, the federal government set minimum eligibility thresholds. Each state could then decide independently whether or not to expand the federal minimums in order to expand the eligible participant base.

One of the goals of the Affordable Care Act was to set the income threshold for Medicaid at 133 percent of the federal poverty level for all states. Some states have eligibility requirements that are more strict than the proposed 133 percent of the federal poverty level. As a result, allowing income up to 133 percent of the federal poverty level, as mandated by the Affordable Care Act, would allow more people to become eligible for Medicaid. In states with expanded, broad eligibility thresholds, like Massachusetts, which is above the 133% threshold, many people who are currently eligible to receive Medicaid funds would become ineligible. In their decision, the Supreme Court ruled that this aspect of the Affordable Care Act was unconstitutional, stating that the decision to expand Medicaid eligibility was a right of state governments, not the federal government. As a result, states will be allowed to opt out of the new eligibility rules set forth by the government. While it remains to be seen which states will opt out of these new rules, if Massachusetts does not, many people who are currently eligible to receive Medicaid funds will become ineligible.

The reason for long-term care planning is simple. First, you need to provide enough assets for the security of your loved ones—they too may have a similar crisis. Second, the rules are extremely complicated and confusing. The result is that without planning and implantation of a plan for protection, many people spend more than they should on long-term care, and their family security is jeopardized.

## IV. Exempt Assets and Countable Assets: What Must Be Spent?

To qualify for Medicaid, applicants must pass some fairly strict tests on the amount of assets they can keep. To understand how Medicaid works, we first need to review what are known as exempt and non-exempt (or countable) assets. Exempt assets are those which Medicaid will not take into account (at least for the time being). In general, the following are the primary exempt assets:

- a home (equity up to $750,000)
  *The home must be the principal place of residence. The nursing home resident may be required to show some "intent to return home," even if this never actually takes place. Caution: The Congressional Budget Office is reviewing the impact of a reduction to $50,000.*

- personal belongings and household goods

- one car or truck

- income-producing real estate

- burial spaces and certain related items for the applicant and spouse

- prepaid funeral accounts

- a pre-need trust (also known as a funeral trust)
  *This is another option for prepaying a funeral.*

- value of life insurance, if face value is $1,500 or less
  *If it does exceed $1,500 in total face amount, then the cash value in these policies is countable.*

All other assets are generally nonexempt and are countable. Basically, all money and property, and any item that can be valued and turned into cash, are countable assets, unless the asset is one of those listed above as exempt.

For example, the following would be considered countable assets:

- cash, savings and checking accounts, and credit union share and draft accounts

- certificates of deposit
- U.S. Savings Bonds
- Individual Retirement Accounts (IRA) and Keogh plans (401(k), 403(b))
- nursing home accounts
- prepaid funeral contracts (which can be canceled)
- trusts (depending on the terms of the trust)
- real estate (other than the primary residence)
- more than one car
- boats or recreational vehicles
- stocks, bonds, or mutual funds
- land contracts or mortgages held on real estate sold

While the Medicaid rules themselves are complicated and tricky, it's safe to say that a single person will qualify for Medicaid as long as he or she has only exempt assets plus a small amount of cash and/or money in the bank (up to $2,000 in Massachusetts).

## V. Some Common Questions

1. Q: I've added my kids' names to our bank account. Do they still count?

   Yes. The entire amount is counted unless you can prove some or all of the money was contributed by the other person who is on the account. This rule applies to cash assets such as:

   - savings and checking accounts
   - credit union share and draft accounts
   - certificates of deposit
   - U.S. Savings Bonds

Note, however, mutual funds from non-bank financial institutions are not subject to this same rule. In other words, the portion contributed by the other person would not be considered an available asset of the "Medicaid Applicant".

2. Q: Can't I just give my assets away?

Many people wonder if they can give their assets away. The answer is, maybe, but only if it's done just right. The law has severe penalties for people who simply give away their assets to create Medicaid eligibility. In Massachusetts, for example, every $8,010 given away during the five years prior to a Medicaid application creates a one-month period of ineligibility. Caution: The Congressional Budget Office is reviewing the impact of an increase from 5 years to 10 years. Another major problem provided by the 2006 legislation is that the penalty period does not begin to run until the Medicaid applicant is in a nursing home and basically out of money, making it impossible to pay for a stay in the nursing home by the penalty period, since there is no money left. So even though the federal gift tax laws allow you to give away up to $14,000 per year without gift tax consequences, such a gift could result in a significant period of ineligibility. Giving under the new rules may be possible; however, it is critically important that you have the advice of an attorney well versed in these new rules.

3. Q: I heard I can give away $14,000 per year. Can I?

As discussed earlier, many people have heard of the federal gift tax provision that allows them to give away $14,000 per year without paying any gift taxes. What they do not know is that this refers to a gift tax exemption. It is not an absolute right where Medicaid is concerned. Having heard of the exemption, they wonder, "Can't I give my assets away?" The answer is, maybe, but only if it's done within the strict allowances of the law. So even though the federal gift tax law allows you to give away up to $14,000 per year, as of January 1, 2013 (up from $13,000), without incurring tax, those gifts could result in a Medicaid period of ineligibility for months. Still, some parents want to make gifts to their children before their life savings is all gone.

25

For more information consider the Case Study "Financial Gifts to Children" in the pages that follow.

Though some families do spend virtually all of their savings on nursing home care, Medicaid often does not require it. There are a number of strategies that can be used to protect family financial security.

# CHAPTER ELEVEN:
## ASSET PROTECTION:
## PLANNING FOR MARRIED COUPLES

There are opportunities available under the Spousal Impoverishment provisions of the Medicare Catastrophic Coverage Act of 1988, but they apply only to couples. The intent of the law was to change the eligibility requirements for Medicaid when one spouse needs nursing home care while the other spouse remains in the community (i.e., at home). The law, in effect, recognizes that it makes little sense to impoverish both spouses when only one needs to qualify for Medicaid assistance for nursing home care.

The couple gathers all their countable assets together in a review. Exempt assets, discussed above, are not counted. The at-home or "community spouse" is allowed to keep countable assets to a maximum of approximately $115,920. The amount of the countable assets that the at-home spouse gets to keep is called the Community Spouse Resource Allowance (CSRA).

Each state also establishes a monthly income for the at-home spouse. This is called the Minimum Monthly Maintenance Needs Allowance. This permits the community spouse to keep a minimum monthly income, ranging to $2,898. If the community spouse does not have at least $1,891.25 in income, then he or she is allowed to take the income of the nursing home spouse in an amount large enough to reach the minimum monthly maintenance needs allowance (i.e., up to at least $2,898). The nursing home spouse's remaining income goes to the nursing home. This avoids the necessity (hopefully) for the at-home spouse to dip into savings each month, which would result in gradual impoverishment. To illustrate, assume the at-home spouse receives $800 per month in social security. Also assume that her needs are calculated to be the minimum of $1,760. With her social security, she is $960 short each month:

> $1,604 at-home spouse's monthly needs (as determined by formula)
>
> $800 at-home spouse's social security
>
> $804 shortfall

In this case, the community spouse will receive $960 (the shortfall amount) per month from the nursing home spouse's social security, and the rest of the nursing home spouse's income will then go to pay for the cost of the nursing home care. This does not mean, however, that there are no planning alternatives that the couple can pursue. Consider the following case studies:

## Case Study: Medicaid Planning for Married People

Ralph and Alice were high school sweethearts who lived in Natick, Massachusetts, their entire adult lives. Two weeks ago, Ralph and Alice celebrated their fifty-first anniversary. Yesterday, Alice, who has Alzheimer's, wandered away from home. Hours later she was found sitting on a curb, talking incoherently. She was taken to a hospital and treated for dehydration. Ralph seeks advice after their family doctor tells him he needs to place Alice in a nursing home. He says they both grew up during the Depression and have always tried to save something every month. Their assets, totaling $200,000, not including their house, are as follows:

| | |
|---|---|
| savings account | $50,000 |
| CDs | 45,000 |
| money market account | 100,000 |
| checking account | 5,000 |

Ralph gets social security and pension checks totaling $1,500 each month; Alice's check is $450. His eyes fill with tears as he says, "At $12,000 to the nursing home every month, our entire life savings will be gone in less than three years!" What's more, he's concerned he won't be able to pay her monthly nursing home bill because a neighbor told him that nursing home will be entitled to all of their social security checks.

There is good news for Ralph and Alice. It's possible he will get to keep his income and most of their assets and still have the state Medicaid program pay Alice's nursing home costs. While the process may take a little while, the end result will be worth it. To apply for Medicaid, he will have to go through MassHealth.

If he does things strictly according to the way MassHealth tells him, he will only be able to keep the CSRA (or about $113,640); in addition he will keep his income. But the results can actually be much better than the traditional spend-down, which everyone talks about. Ralph might be able to turn the spend-down amount of roughly $100,000 into an income stream for him that will increase his income and meet the Medicaid spend down virtually right away. In other words, if handled properly Alice may be eligible for MassHealth from the first month that she goes into the nursing home. Please note this will not work in every case. This is why it is important to have an elder law attorney guide you through the system and the Medicaid process to find the strategies that will be most beneficial in your situation.

So, Ralph will have to get advice from someone who knows how to navigate the system. But with proper advice, he may be able to keep most of what he and Alice have worked so hard for. This is possible because the law does not intend to impoverish one spouse because the other needs care in a nursing home. This is certainly an example where knowledge of the rules and how to apply them can be used to resolve Ralph and Alice's dilemma. Of course, proper Medicaid planning differs according to the relevant facts and circumstances of each situation as well as the state law.

## Case Study: A Trust for a Disabled Child

Margaret and Sam have always taken care of their daughter, Elizabeth. She is forty-five, has never worked, and has never left home. She is developmentally disabled and receives SSI (Supplemental Security Income). They have always worried about

29

who would take care of her after they die. Some years ago, Sam was diagnosed with dementia. His health has deteriorated to the point that Margaret can no longer take care of him. Now she has placed Sam in a nursing home and is paying $4,000 per month out of savings. Margaret is even more worried that there will not be any money left for the care of Elizabeth. Margaret is satisfied with the nursing home Sam is in. The facility has a Medicaid bed available that Sam could have if he were eligible. Medicaid would pay his bill. However, according to the information she got from the social worker, Sam is $48,000 away from Medicaid eligibility. Margaret wishes there was a way to save the $48,000 for Elizabeth after she and Sam are gone.

There is. Margaret can consult an elder law attorney to set up a "special needs trust" with the $48,000 to provide for Elizabeth. As soon as Margaret transfers the money to the trust, Sam will be eligible for Medicaid. Elizabeth won't lose her benefits, and her security is assured.

Of course, all trusts must be reviewed for compliance with Medicaid rules. Also, failure to report assets is fraud, and when discovered, will cause loss of eligibility and repayment of benefits and perhaps even criminal penalties. Still, some people question making gifts before entering a nursing home.

## Case Study: Financial Gifts to Children

After her seventy-three-year-old husband, Harold, suffers a paralyzing stroke, Mildred and her daughter, Joan, need advice. Dark circles have formed under Mildred's eyes. Her hair is disheveled. Joan holds her hand. "The doctor says Harold needs long-term care in a nursing home," Mildred says. "I have some money in savings, but not enough. I don't want to lose my house and all our hard-earned money. I don't know what to do."

Joan has heard about Medicaid benefits for nursing homes, but doesn't want her mother left destitute in order for Harold to qualify for them. Joan wants to ensure that her father's medical needs are met, but she also wants to preserve Mildred's assets. "Can't Mom just give her money to me as a gift?" she asks. "Can't she give away $13,000 a year? I could keep the money for her so she doesn't lose it when Dad applies for Medicaid."

Joan has confused general estate and tax laws with the issue of asset transfers and Medicaid eligibility. A gift to a child in this case is actually a transfer, and Medicaid has very specific rules about transfers. At the time Harold applies for Medicaid, for gifts made prior to February 8, 2006, the state will look back three years to see if any gifts have been made. Gifts made after February 8, 2006 will be subject to a five-year look-back. The state won't let you just give away your money or your property to qualify for Medicaid. Any gifts or transfers for less than fair market value that are uncovered in the look-back period will cause a delay in Harold's eligibility for Medicaid. In addition to the changes in the look-back period from three to five years, the new law also states that the penalty period on asset transfers will not begin until the Medicaid applicant is in the nursing home and already spent down to $2,000 in countable assets. This will frustrate the gifting plans of most people.

So what can Harold and Mildred do? They may be able to institute a gifting program, save a good portion of their estate, and still qualify for Medicaid. But they have to set it up just right. The new rules are very "nit-picky." You should consult a knowledgeable advisor on how this may be accomplished.

# CHAPTER TWELVE:
# WILL I LOSE MY HOME?

Many people who apply for Medicaid assistance benefits to pay for nursing home care ask this question. For many, the home constitutes much or most of their life savings. Often, it's the only asset that a person has to pass on to his or her children. Under the Medicaid regulations, the home is an exempt asset (so long as equity is less than $750,000). This means that it is not taken into account when calculating eligibility for Medicaid. But in 1993, Congress passed a little-debated law that affects hundreds of thousands of families with a spouse or elderly parent in a nursing home. That law requires states to try to recover the value of Medicaid payments made to nursing home residents. Estate recovery does not take place until the recipient of the benefits dies (or until both spouses are deceased if it is a married couple). Then, federal law requires that states attempt to recover the benefits paid from the recipient's probate and in some cases non-probate estate. Generally, the probate estate consists of assets that the deceased owned in his or her name alone without beneficiary designation. The non-probate assets include assets owned jointly or payable to a beneficiary.

One new major concern is the Congressional Budget Office (CBO) considering the impact of reducing the exemption for home equity value to $50,000. If this happens this means that most homes will no longer be exempt. Therefore, most people will have to act in advance to protect their homes. Under current law there is some opportunity for married couples who haven't planned in advance to utilize the home exemption. However, the reduction to $50,000 from the current $750,000 will all but eliminate this emergency planning strategy for married couples.

Another problem exists in that if the nursing home resident gets too sick to return home, a lien will be placed on the home and the home eventually sold to pay back nursing home costs paid on behalf of the nursing home resident as well as future nursing home costs. There are better alternatives which enable you to protect your home so it will not be sold at auction to pay nursing home bills. But you must act quickly as the CBO is also studying the impact of changing the look-back period from 5 to 10 years.

About two-thirds of the nation's nursing home residents have their costs paid in part by Medicaid. Today, the estate recovery law affects many families. The asset most frequently caught in the estate recovery web is the home of the Medicaid recipient. A nursing home resident can often own a home and receive Medicaid benefits without having to sell the home. But upon death, if the home is part of the probate estate, the state may seek to force the sale of the home in order to reimburse the state for the payments that were made. Since Medicaid rules are constantly changing, you will need assistance from someone knowledgeable about these rules.

# CHAPTER THIRTEEN:
## HOW TO USE "SECRET DOLLARS" TO PAY FOR LONG-TERM CARE

## I. Veteran's Benefit for Long-Term Care Revealed

Thousands of Massachusetts veterans may not be receiving the Veterans Administration (VA) disability benefits they are entitled to. One of the VA's best-kept secrets, which is an excellent potential source of funds for long-term care are veteran's benefits for a *non-service connected disability*. Most VA benefits and pensions are based on a disability that was incurred during a veteran's wartime service. However, this particular benefit is available for individuals who are disabled due to the issues of old age, such as Alzheimer's, Parkinson's, multiple sclerosis, and other physical disabilities, and have the additional requirement of needing the aid and attendance of another person in order to avoid the hazards of his or her daily environment. What that means in English is the veteran needs someone to help him or her prepare meals, bathe, dress, and otherwise take care of him- or herself. These benefits can be a blessing for the eligible disabled individual who is not yet ready for a nursing home.

Under this program, a veteran, not married to another veteran, can receive *a maximum of $2,053 per month* in benefits, and a widow can receive *up to $1,112 per month*. A single veterans is entitled to a benefit of $1,731 per month.

In order to qualify for these "secret dollars," the applicant must be "permanently and totally disabled" based on VA standards. The applicant does not need to be helpless—he or she need only show that he/she is in need of aid and attendance on a regular basis. A person who is housebound or in an assisted-living facility and is over the age of sixty-five is presumed by the VA to be in need of aid and attendance. We were shocked to learn that thousands of Massachusetts veterans in need may be missing out on this valuable benefit that they have a legal right to receive.

## II. Filing a Claim for Veteran's Benefits

To file a claim for this benefit, it is wise to seek the involvement of a trained veteran's service officer. A veteran's service officer is critical to the filing of an application with the local VA regional office. It is also important to seek the guidance of an experienced elder law attorney who is familiar with estate planning, disability, Medicaid, and veterans' benefits.

## III. Do You Qualify for "Secret Dollars"?

This particular program does have substantial limitations related to the income and assets that are held by the applicant. However, the countable income for veterans' benefits is determined by taking an individual's gross income and *subtracting* from that *all* of the individual's unreimbursed medical expenses to determine his or her Income for Veteran Administration Purposes (IVAP), which is ultimately used to determine whether or not the person qualifies.

Some of the cost of an assisted living facility, and even some of the cost of an independent living facility, may also be an allowable medical deduction to reduce a veteran's gross income to a much lower net countable income that may qualify him or her for veterans' benefits. It is very important to meet with a knowledgeable veteran's service officer or an experienced elder law attorney for a pre-filing consultation to determine whether or not a veteran may qualify. It is also important to review the estate planning work to see what may be done to assist the veteran in qualifying for this particular benefit. There may be planning steps that can be implemented before applying that will help a veteran or widow to qualify and/or obtain an *increased* benefit.

Determining what the countable income is, as measured by the VA, is very confusing to many individuals. An attorney skilled in elder

35

law can provide a veteran and the veteran's family with appropriate pre-filing consultations to determine the correct steps that must be taken to be able to determine if it would be right to apply for this VA benefit. Please contact our firm, The Estate Planning & Asset Protection Law Center of Dennis Sullivan & Associates, for more information or for asset protection analysis. You can call us at (781) 237-2815. The professionals at the firm have experience helping counsel senior citizens and their families in the area of elder law, including estate planning, disability, Medicaid planning, and veterans' benefits related to long-term care needs. Additional information is also available at www.SullivanVeteransReport.com.

# CHAPTER FOURTEEN:
# NURSING HOME ALTERNATIVES: PLAN AHEAD FOR A PROTECTED LIFESTYLE

Nursing home care is expensive and often unwanted. When asked, people overwhelmingly say that they would prefer to stay at home. In fact, in a study conducted by the Society of Actuaries, 38% of women and 26% of men surveyed stated they were concerned about not being able to stay at home in their later years. Fortunately, there are a number of alternatives to nursing homes including: At Home Care, Specialized At Home Care, Independent Living Facilities, Assisted Living Facilities, and Continuing Care Retirement Communities, and Adult Day Health Centers.

This chapter on alternatives to nursing home care will be a helpful resource to people and their families as they plan for and evaluate their future lifestyle and long term care and living options. The information provided in this chapter has been enhanced by the Choices for Care Study Program (www.ChoiceforCare.com) developed by Chip Kessler, who provided the forward for this guide.

## I. At Home Health Care
### Type I– Non-Medically Trained Home Health Care Aid

When considering whether or not at home care is appropriate for you or your loved one, consider the specific type of care as well as the services a home health care provider can offer as well as the individual's specific needs. There are two types of at home health care providers, home health aids and home care by medically trained professionals such as a registered nurse.

The first type of providers are often referred to as home health aids. The care provider is not medically trained, though they have received 3-4 hours of orientation training on the needs of their clients. This orientation is likely provided by the person/company that owns and operates the home care agency you are contracting with. Under the law, a home healthcare provider is only allowed to give "medication reminders". The caregiver will remind the individual that it is time to take their medication, but they are not permitted to physically handle or dispense any medication.

Typical at home care services generally include:
- Personal Grooming
  - bathing, hygiene care, toileting, and incontinence care
- Household Functions
  - Preparing meals, feeding assistance, and housework
- Running Errands
- Travel
  - Providing a means of transportation
- Companionship
  - Accompanying the individual to restaurants, movies, plays, events
  - In home activities such as reading out loud or playing cards

At home health care is generally done in shifts of no less than 4 hours for 24 hours, for a specified number of days per week. The schedule is flexible and the individual is free to select what days they need assistance.

If you are considering at home care, it is advisable to visit one or more of your local at home health care agencies. You should meet with these companies so that you can get a sense of what type of care the company will provide, the background of the organization, and the staff that will be providing the in home services. You will want to know:

- The training at home care givers receive
- The exact services the agency offers
- Does the agency perform background checks on in home care providers before hiring them
- Is the agency licensed, bonded, and insured
- References from people/families the agency is currently providing care for

The cost for at home care services varies. The differences are based on location and the type of services needed. The average nationwide is between $15 and $19 per hour. Massachusetts has several Community Resource Programs available to help people coordinate and pay for their care without going broke. Our team of professionals has helped a number of families determine which program is right for them. Each person and situation is unique. We can even help families determine the level of care they may need based on their current health and financial situations. To learn more call our office at (781) 237-2815.

## II. At Home Health Care
### Type II - Specialized at Home Care Services – Medically Trained, Licensed & Certified Individuals

Specialized at home care is a more unique form of home health care. It's only available with a doctor's order to patients who qualify to pay for this service in the following means:

- Medicare
- Managed Care/Private Insurance
- Private Pay

With Specialized Care at Home, a Licensed Practical Nurse (LPN) or a Registered Nurse (RN) visits the person's home that is in need of the care and services. The skill level that is required to take care of the person's needs determines whether the provider will be an RN or an LPN assigned to the case.

The nurse works under the direction and orders of the individual's personal physician. The RN or LPN will come to a person's private residence as determined by the level and frequency of care the individual requires. The specialized care nurse's main duty is to instruct and educate the individual (and perhaps you as well if we're talking about a loved one or close friend) on providing at home care. Here you and/or a loved one learn how to best deal with particular care needs and provide proper attention.

In addition to nurses, the specialized at home care agency can provide Registered Physical Therapists and Licensed Physical Therapy Assistants for similar home visits. The physical therapists or physical therapy assistants will:

- Develop and implement exercise programs
- Provide heat and ultrasound treatments
- Offer other services as needed

In addition, the specialized care agency will offer Registered Occupational Therapists, or Certified Occupational Therapy Assistants, to assist with daily activities of living such as showering and grooming to promote maximum independence at home.

In addition, the Specialized at Home Care agency may offer Speech/Language Pathologists to provide therapy. Here the goal is restoring or improving verbal communication skills.

As with regular at home healthcare (see above) you and the Specialized at Home Care agency work together to set up a home visitation schedule for any nurse, physical or occupational therapy services as needed and required. The same scheduling partnership holds true if there is a need for a Speech/Language Pathologist.

Because your loved one will be working with Registered Nurses and/or Licensed Practical Nurses, he or she can receive medication directly from the nurse, an important distinction from regular at home health care.

Cost for Specialized at home care is greater than regular at home health care services because of the nature of the care and services offered. Again, you or a loved one must have a doctor's order to receive specialized at home care services, and meet specific payment criteria. Payment options include:

- Medicare (if you or the person receiving the care is eligible)
- Managed Care or Private Insurance
- Private Pay

It is recommended that if specialized at home care sounds like something you are interested in that you then contact one or several of those organizations offering this caregiving option in your region and community. You may want to also speak with the attending physician as he or she will be writing the order for this specific form of care. The physician may also have some recommendations regarding a specific specialized at home care company.

## III. Independent Living Facility

Moving to an independent living facility is the first option that involves a person moving from their present home to a new location. If this thought troubles you, you can take comfort in the fact that many people consider the act of moving as a natural part of life. It is usually done because of practical reasons such as a new job, a transfer to a new location, a desire to live in a more inviting climate, to be closer to family and/or friends, or for a healthcare related situation and need. You can look at the act of moving in this case as a positive and pro-active action to meet the situation at hand as it is presented.

As its title states, an independent living facility is the mode of residency that offers the most "hands off treatment" of all the nursing home alternatives profiled in this chapter. The independent living environment appeals to people who wish to enjoy a lifestyle filled with recreational, social and educational activities, yet live in a setting that offers the security and conveniences that are found in this group sector. Independent Living accommodations are generally

41

called "suites" and resemble smaller style apartments and/or condominiums. The suites come complete with a kitchen, bathroom, living room, closets and a bedroom. Some suites may even feature two bedrooms and are priced accordingly. There is generally no sharing of a suite unless specifically requested by the parties that would be living in it.

Some Independent Living Communities do offer recreational activities such as:

- Pool
- Exercise room
- Clubhouse or a lounge
- Day room that can be used for birthday parties and/or family get togethers
- Library/reading room
- Other Independent Living Facility services may include:
  - o Laundry room
  - o Meals in a facility dining room or access to meals
  - o Housekeeping Services
  - o Indoor and/or outdoor recreational activities
  - o Social Activities
  - o Educational activities
  - o Transportation services to things such as doctor's appointments or shopping malls.

When considering moving to an independent living facility it is important to keep in mind that very often no medical or healthcare staff is on the premises. Certain Independent Living staff may or may not be trained in CPR. As a result of this lack of available medical assistance there in generally no help given with medication or any personal/physical needs such as help with walking, toileting or incontinence care.

Independent Living Facilities, unlike Assisted Living Centers and Nursing Homes, are not licensed either on the local, state or federal level and are not formally regulated. As a result the management company or entity running the building sets all the rules and regulations for the operation of the facility.

An important note about caregiving services in the Independent Living setting: Because your suite in the Independent Living Facility is considered your private home, you are eligible to receive either of the home health care services or the specialized at home care services profiled earlier in this chapter. You are encouraged to refer back to those sections for a thorough understanding of the type of care and services the home health care options offer. Check with your local Independent Living Facility to find out if it can assist in arranging any home health care services, or if this is something you would have to do on your own. Remember too that home healthcare services and their costs are separate from the cost of residing in an Independent Living Facility.

The fee for residing in an Independent Living Community depends upon the state and local location of the establishment and the amount of amenities and services offered. Those living in this setting pay all expenses as no third-party payment options are accepted. Contact your local Independent Living Facilities to see if they require any kind of lease agreement or if they will allow a month-to-month rental basis.

If what you've read about Independent Living Facilities has sparked your interest in the Independent Living Facility environment, it is recommended that you visit one of more of these type of buildings in your community and region. You may also want to consider making your first contact over the telephone to obtain some preliminary information.

One additional suggestion regarding any in-person visits you are planning to make: consider making a follow-up visit to the facility or facilities at a different time of the day and a different day of the week than your first visit. This will allow you to observe the facility at different points of the week and with potentially different staff on the premises. Doing this will give you the opportunity to gain different perspectives and help you in the decision making process in determining if the Independent Living lifestyle is your best option.

One other note here of interest: definitely consider making one, or all, of your in-person visits to a facility unannounced. You do not have to feel it is necessary to schedule an appointment. Independent Living Facilities are used to people dropping in. All facilities should have more than one individual available to give you a tour and/or answer your questions. If a particular facility does not, this should tell you something.

## IV. Assisted Living

Assisted Living care and services provide a more modest form of supervised structure that can meet the needs of many residents and their families. Assisted Living care and services generally fall in between the "hands-off" approach of Independent Living Facilities and the intensive nature of Nursing Home caregiving. Assisted Living care is not based on around-the-clock, one-on-one caregiving services. As such, staff is there to work with and assist those that reside in the building. Assisted Living staff often includes Certified Nursing Assistants (CNA's) and Licensed Practical Nurses (LPN's). One note of special interest regarding Assisted Living staff: a registered nurse (RN) may or may not be on the Assisted Living Center staff. Many Assisted Living Facilities however, do employ a Registered Nurse to serve as the building's Director of Nursing.

Assisted Living care and services generally include:

- Reminders from staff on medications
  - o The exact level of assistance on medication differs from state-to-state based on state regulations.

- Care Plan Conferences
  - o This is where the staff, family and resident get together to formulate a "plan of care" that best suits the resident's needs. The goal here is for all parties to work together to insure a reasonably satisfying stay

44

for the resident within the Assisted Living Community. Usually there is a Care Plan conference held shortly after the new resident arrives, with periodic follow-up meetings throughout the resident's stay in the facility. The resident and/or family can request a follow-up Care Plan conference when they believe the situation warrants.

- Physical, Speech and Occupational Therapy and Rehabilitation services available in many Assisted Living Communities
- Meal Service
- Help with dressing, grooming, bathing, laundry and other daily activities as requested
- Housekeeping Services
- Group Outings
- Daily Recreational Activities
- Pet Therapy
- Beauty and Barber Shop Services
- Alzheimer's/Dementia Unit.
  - o This may be a special wing of the facility complete with specific staff trained to work with residents who need this special and unique form of caregiving assistance

Living accommodations within the Assisted Living environment are usually broken down into one or two possibilities:

- Private suites/units which may or may not have a separate bedroom; in some cases a larger "living area" may also house both a sofa, a chair and a bed.
- Shared quarters with another resident. In this case the suite/unit would feature two separate bedrooms.

Assisted Living suites usually feature a kitchenette with a refrigerator and a microwave oven. Here residents would enjoy the opportunity to prepare small meals on their own.

Assisted Living Communities are licensed and regulated at the state level. Each state governs these facilities based on its own regulations. Each facility, based on location is inspected once per year to once every few years as mandated by its home state criteria. State surveyors conduct these unannounced surprise inspections. The inspections are done with consumer in mind to make sure the Assisted Living Center is complying with state health and safety rules and regulations. Nationally the track record of most Assisted Living Communities shows them to be operating in a safe and a professional manner.

Costs for Assisted Living Community care and services vary based on the number of services and the type of accommodations offered (i.e. private versus shared quarters). A select few states accept third-party payment programs such as Medicaid and Medicare. Check with any of your local Assisted Living Communities to see what if any Federal and/or State government payment partners are accepted and the criteria a facility resident must meet for eligibility. Other payment options may include:

- Long-Term Care Insurance
- Private pay

Each Assisted Living Community has on staff an individual trained to work with the new resident and his or her family/responsible party on all payment matters. Please feel free to consult with this person regarding any questions you may have.

If you are considering a move to an Assisted Living Facility for you or a loved one, it is strongly suggested that you plan an in-person visit to one or more such facilities. Nothing beats an in-person visit in order to see first-hand what an Assisted Living Facility has to offer. It is also recommended that you visit more than one time.

Make your initial visit during peak time, Monday-Friday 9 a.m. through 5 p.m. Then plan to re-visit during the evening and/or the weekend. This way, you will get a feel for the building's operation during different parts of a day and the week. You will also get to see different staff on-the-job as well. Regarding any in-person visits you are planning, it's also recommended that you make them unannounced to best further your learning process.

It is also critical to carefully read the Assisted Living Facility's contract and review the leases and legal documents to see exactly what services are going to be provided and at what cost. There is a wide range of services provided by different facilities, so it is very important that you know and understand what assistance you or your loved one are going to be provided. These details should be spelled out in the contract, lease, and service agreement.

## V. Continuing Care Retirement Communities

Continuing care retirement communities (CCRCs) are communities that provide a full continuum of care for their residents. They have flexible accommodations designed to meet their residents' health and housing needs as their needs change over time. CCRC facilities usually offer independent living, assisted living and nursing home care services, all under one roof.

As a requirement for admission to most CCRCs, residents are required to pay an entrance fee or a lump sum "buy-in", which guarantees the residents' the right to live in the facility for the remainder of their lifetime. The entrance fee ranges from $200,000-$600,000 with an additional monthly fee, which can vary from $2,500 to $6,000 per month or more.

The entrance fee is often reimbursable if the resident decides to leave the facility, if the resident passes away while at the facility or if the resident terminates their contract with the facility. Additionally, many contracts allow the resident to use some or all of the entrance fee to pay for the monthly resident charges if they become financially unable to pay otherwise.

You should be careful of committing all your savings to paying an entrance fee for a CCRC. In 2009, Erickson Retirement

Communities, which was operating in CCRCs in 10 states, including Massachusetts, filed for bankruptcy. Although Erickson was able to emerge from debt after restructuring its debt, there remains a chance that if you put all your life savings into paying a CCRC entrance fee, the operator could go bankrupt and leave you with nothing.

Before the new Medicaid Law, these entrance fees were not considered countable assets. Since 2005 however, the entrance fee will be considered a countable asset by Medicaid if (1) the contract provides that the entrance fee may be used to pay for care should the resident run out of money and become unable to pay the monthly charge; (2) the individual is eligible for a refund of any remaining entrance fee when the individual dies, leaves the community, or otherwise terminates the life contract; and (3) the entrance fee does not give the resident an ownership interest in the CCRC.

CCRCs, under the Medicaid laws in place since 2005, are given the authority to include in their contracts a provision that requires residents to spend all of their resources on their care before applying for Medicaid, essentially disallowing any Medicaid planning or asset protection planning once the contract is signed.

When an individual applies for admission to a CCRC, the application requires full disclosure of an individual's resources. The CCRCs are allowed to contractually prohibit an individual from doing long term care or asset protection planning, requiring instead that they spend down all their assets before applying to Medicaid. This effectively limits the ability of CCRC residents to protect their assets once they have been admitted to a facility.

## VI. Adult Day Health Centers

An Adult Day Health Center is a wonderful alternative to families struggling with the care of an aging or disabled parent, spouse, or loved one. Adult Day Health Centers can provide supervision and assistance each day for a senior who is not quite ready for an assisted living or nursing home facility.

Each center has a staff of trained health care professionals, including registered nurses and therapists, to help those with complex physical or psychological problems and needs. Adult Day Health Centers provide a structured program that includes a variety of health, social, and supportive services in a safe, protective environment.

Services are provided during the daytime, allowing caregiver's peace of mind if they need to continue working. They also provide much needed respite for caregivers so their able to face the challenges associated with day-today caregiving.

Members of Adult Day Health Centers can look forward to a variety of challenging, interesting, and entertaining activities each day. Their caregivers can feel confident that excellent medical and therapeutic care will be provided by an experienced staff of health care professionals. Most centers provide a light breakfast, lunch, and an afternoon snack.

For those individuals who meet the requirements, Medicaid, the VA and other funded programs cover Adult Day Health Centers services. Long term care insurance policies may also cover the cost of an Adult Day Health Centers facility. If you have a long term care policy, it is important to examine your policy carefully.

## VII. Summary

The different types of lifestyle and long term care alternatives include (1) at home care provided by a home health care aid; (2) at home care provided by a medically trained professional; (3) independent living facilities; (4) assisted living facilities; (5) Continuing Care Retirement Communities; and (6) Adult Day Health Centers. The decision on what is best given your unique situation often will depend on the results of a Strategy Session and Care Giver Blue Print. Our care coordinator can even help your family determine what services are needed now and what will likely be needed in the future. This Strategy Session and Care Giver Blue Print is often useful in helping you determine how your financial circumstances will be impacted by your potential long term care needs. In our experience, those who plan ahead have the most flexible options available to them when important decisions need to be made. This is why planning in advance is so critically important. To learn more about how our team can help you or your loved one with a home Strategy Session and Care Giver Blue Print or a review of your financial situation, please call (781) 237-2815.

At the Estate Planning & Asset Protection Law Center of Dennis Sullivan & Associates, we help people and their families concerned with losing their homes and life savings to increasing medical and nursing home costs, taxes and the costs and time delays of probate. We also protect clients from losing control of their own health and financial decisions.

If you would like to learn more about our process and what you can do to enhance the security of your spouse, home, life savings and legacy you can register for a seat at an upcoming workshop by calling (800) 964-4295 (24/7) or registering online.

# CHAPTER FIFTEEN:
## ETHICAL CONSIDERATIONS

Professionals have certain fiduciary responsibilities to act in the best interests of their clients they represent. The term *fiduciary* refers to a relationship of confidence or trust between two or more parties. A fiduciary is one who acts on behalf of another, giving rise to a special relationship of trust and confidence. When working with senior clients, a practitioner often serves clients in a fiduciary capacity.

The duties a fiduciary owes to his or her clients are broad. They include honesty and integrity, full disclosure, loyalty, good faith, and fairness. As a practical matter, they also require that a practitioner:

- act in the best interest of the client;
- make product recommendations that best serve the client's needs;
- honestly and accurately represent the features; and
- consider the concerns of other family members but always being mindful that they must first serve the needs and objectives of the client, most often the senior.

As the level of professionalism increases, so does the level of expected service; as the expected level of service increases, so does the required standard of practice and responsibility. A practitioner is required to apply the level of care and service that is obtained through specialized knowledge, training, skills, and experience.

When working with senior clients, the professional should be aware of the need to make sure that he or she is communicating effectively and in a manner the client can understand. An important part of a professional's duty to his or her clients is to provide ongoing reviews of the plan that was created. The professional who has assured his or her client that their planning is adequate has a duty to periodically review that coverage, in light of the client's changing situation, and to suggest additional coverage if necessary.

In addition to guaranteed education and value at the Estate Planning and Asset Protection Law Center, we provide the Lifetime Protection Program. Members of the program are provided a yearly review of their personal, health and financial situations to be sure that their plan continues to accomplish their goals and objectives. This is especially important with all the changes health care and tax laws as well as personal and financial situations. We provide a free one-year membership in the Lifetime Protection Program, for all new clients when they join, so they can experience the value of maintaining up-to-date plans that will achieve their goals and objectives, even as the law and personal circumstances continue to change. To find out more about the Lifetime Protection Program, call our office at (781) 237-2815 or review the program online at www.DSullivan.com/Lifetime-Protection-Program.

# CHAPTER SIXTEEN:
# LEGAL ASSISTANCE

Aging persons and their family members face many unique legal issues. As you can tell from our discussion of the Medicaid and Medicare programs, the legal, financial, and care planning issues facing the prospective nursing home resident and family can be particularly complex. If you or a family member needs nursing home care, it is clear that you need legal help. Where can you turn for that help?

It is difficult for the consumer to be able to identify lawyers who have the training and experience required to provide guidance during this most difficult time. Generally, nursing home planning and Medicaid planning are aspects of the services provided by elder law attorneys. Consumers must be cautious in choosing a lawyer and carefully investigate the lawyer's credentials. How do you find a law office that has the knowledge and experience you need?

You may want to start with recommendations from friends who have received professional help with nursing home issues. Who did they use? Were they satisfied with the services they received? Hospital social workers, Alzheimer and other support groups, and accountants and other financial professionals can also be good sources of recommendations.

In general, lawyers who devote a substantial part of their practice to nursing home planning should have more knowledge and experience to address the issues properly. Don't hesitate to ask the lawyer what percentage of his or her practice involves nursing home planning.

Ask whether the lawyer is a member of any elder law planning organizations. Does the lawyer provide workshops on nursing home planning, and if so, to whom? (For example, if the lawyer is asked to teach other about elder law, nursing home and Veteran's Benefit

53

planning, it is a very good sign that the lawyer is considered to be knowledgeable by people who should know.) If the lawyer volunteers to provide community education, you might try to attend one of the workshops. This should help you decide if this is the lawyer for you.

In the end, follow your instincts and choose an attorney who knows this area of the law, who is committed to helping others, and who will listen to you and the unique wants and needs of you and your family.

At The Estate Planning & Asset Protection Law Center of Dennis Sullivan & Associates, we are attorneys and CPAs who are members of four national organizations so we can continue to learn more about the best new ways to help people and their families in this critically important area for us all, now and in the years ahead. These organizations include the Life Care Planning Law Firm Association, ElderCounsel, the National Academy of Elder Law Attorneys, and WealthCounsel. If you are concerned for yourself or your loved one and wish to learn more, we offer educational seminars for the community that discuss Medicaid planning and other estate planning and asset protection concerns. We encourage you to attend one of our free educational workshops to learn more about our process and what you can do to enhance the security of your spouse, home, life savings, and legacy. To register for a seat at an upcoming workshop call (800) 964-4295 (24–7) or register online at www.DSullivan.com. For those who are home bound, resources are available online and workshops are available on DVD. These DVDs provide the same important information on how you can assess you situation today and plan for a protected future, which will help increase peace of mind for you and your family.

# ADDITIONAL RESOURCES

1. www.BostonSeniorResources.com/Cut-Nursing-Home-Costs

   What you don't know about paying for a nursing home could cost you everything. Discover the seven steps you should be taking RIGHT NOW to get quality long-term care without going broke.

2. www.SullivanVeteransReport.com

   Are you or a loved one a veteran? Discover if you qualify for a little know veteran's benefit that could provide as much a $2,053 per month for your long-term care. Thousands of Massachusetts veterans are missing out. Don't be one of them.

3. www.BostonMemoryLawyer.com

   Discover the ninety-two most significant, hard-to-find breakthroughs in Alzheimer's care in the *Complete Alzheimer's Resource Kit*. The kit includes care tips from master Alzheimer's caregiver, Jo Huey. The kit has answers to difficult financial questions and a legal survival guide no family dealing with Alzheimer's should be without.

4. www.DSullivan.com

   On our website we have made available several guides, reports, case studies, and videos that are designed to help people and their families understand how to plan for a protected future. We also have a helpful blog with new information and helpful articles added frequently.

5. Other Books Written By the Professionals at the Estate Planning & Asset Protection Law Center

   - *Generations: Planning Your Legacy*

- *Legacy: Plan, Protect and Preserve Your Estate*

- *Living and Learning: Achieve Retirement and Income Security*

- *Estate Planning Strategies: Collective Wisdom. Proven Techniques.*

- *The Trustee Manual: A Family Trustee Resource*

# BONUS CHAPTER

## CASE STUDIES: FAILING TO PLAN AND EMERGENCY PLANNING

### Case Study One. The Lawrence Family Case Study: Failure to Plan Costs Thousands

The Lawrence Family initially contacted our office looking for help, which prevented them from making a very costly mistake. They were confused because they were told that they should deed their home to the children. Like many people we have helped, their home was their largest asset. When asked if they liked the idea of their children paying $150,000 in unnecessary capital gains on the sale of the home, they said of course they did not. With our advice, the Mr. & Mrs. Lawrence decided not to transfer their home to the children, avoiding that expensive MISTAKE. Instead, when they sold the home, the sale was tax-free and the proceeds were added to their life savings.

### Failure to Plan...A Costly Mistake

Unfortunately for the family, they did not follow our other strong recommendation at the time and for a number of years thereafter, to protect their life savings from being spent down on long term care costs. As a result of their failure to plan ahead, their life savings had to be used to pay $16,000 a month to a care facility, a cost that Mr. Lawrence and Mrs. Lawrence incurred when they both ended up in the same long term care community. Mr. Lawrence was in the nursing home and Mrs. Lawrence was across the courtyard in assisted living.

Although $16,000 per month may seem high, by today's standards Mr. and Mrs. Lawrence would be paying a lot more. Today, nursing home care for ONE person in the Greater Boston area costs an average of $12,000 to $15,000 per month. This cost is completely avoidable however, and could have been avoided if Mr. & Mrs. Lawrence had come to us in advance. They could've protected everything and even passed the Medicaid 5 year look back period.

## It's Never Too Late, Emergency Planning is Possible

All was not lost for Mr. & Mrs. Lawrence however. Fortunately their son and daughter came to us in time to help the family with some advanced asset protection planning before everything was gone. Both children lived out of town, one in Oregon and the other in Europe. But we had a chance to meet with the family before Mr. Lawrence passed away. Our team of professionals was able to help protect $500,000 for Mrs. Lawrence from being forced to be spent on her long term care costs. Because of our successful emergency planning to help the family, we enabled Mrs. Lawrence to remain in assisted living, which is not paid for by Medicaid. She was able to keep additional funds for living expenses and medical expenses, which would otherwise have been paid to the nursing home for Mr. Lawrence's care. Needless to say, at this time of crisis when Mr. Lawrence was in his last days, the family was relieved with the results they accomplished.

## Are Increased Medicaid Look Back Periods on the Horizon?

Long term care planning is a very confusing area, especially with the new health care reform, but all families' have an opportunity to plan ahead in order to comply with the current Medicaid program's 5 year look back. It should be noted that it is critically important for people to get their planning done now. The look back period was increased from 3 to 5 years in 2006, and many are now speculating that another increase somewhere in the neighborhood of 8 to 10 years. The Congressional Budget Office has been studying the impact on the federal budget of increasing the look back period from

5 to 10 years. Today the law is that everything can be protected within 5 years, so families are not forced to spend their life savings, lose their home, and impoverish their spouse to pay for a nursing home. In most scenarios, planning ahead of the five-year look back is much more effective.

## Case Study Two. The Henry Family Case Study: What Happens if Your Disability Documents Are Not Up to Date

The following case study is illustrates the importance of having up to date health care and disability documents. As part of every estate plan, one should have the documents necessary to allow family members to make your health care and financial decisions if you are ever rendered unable to do so. If you do not have the up to date disability documents, you and your family will be forced to spend wait until the court process is complete to get a guardian and conservator appointed. This can take considerable time and cost your family thousands of dollars.

## Mrs. Henry. Case Study

Mrs. Henry came to our office with a major issue. Her husband, Mr. Henry, had slipped and hit his head very hard. Since that time, Mrs. Henry told us, her husband had been in a persistent vegetative state for nearly 3 months. Mr. Henry, a professional only in his 60's, had not signed the proper health care and disability documents prior to his fall and as a result, Mrs. Henry was not allowed to make any decisions or take any actions on behalf of her husband. Important medical decisions were being left up to a team of doctors who had never met Mr. Henry and had no idea of what he would have wanted. Mrs. Henry wanted to be able to make decisions on her husband's behalf, but the law prevented that.

After listening to this tragic story, we had to tell Mrs. Henry that the only thing she could do at this point was file the necessary paperwork and go to court to have her appointed as temporary guardian and conservator for her husband. There would also be a court review in connection with the application for a temporary and permanent guardianship and conservatorship. The process would involve the preparation of detailed forms and then going to Court to file the documents and plead the case before a judge. We would also be required to make sure all the forms will completed properly, so that the court would accept them. The filing would also result in sensitive private information, like medical records and financial information, being made public record through the Court.

The process for appointing Mrs. Henry as temporary guardian and conservator took several weeks. Like most people, Mrs. Henry and her family were unaware of this lengthy legal process, which can be completely avoided by having the up to date documents signed in advance. If Mr. Henry had simply signed the appropriate paperwork, Mrs. Henry would have been able to immediately consult with her husband's doctors and the hospital on all necessary decisions. Instead, she was forced to spend unnecessary time and money getting herself appointed as guardian and conservator so that she could get Mr. Henry moved to a facility that provided the appropriate level of care so he could begin his rehabilitation and recovery.

At the Estate Planning & Asset Protection Law Center proper health care and disability documents are included with every estate plan. This ensures that our clients have the peace of mind of knowing that should an unspeakable tragedy occur, their family will be able to make important decisions without the need to go to Court, wasting time and money. We even provide a service through which our clients' emergency contact information as well as important disability documents are available to them 24/7. No matter where they are, if something happens, knowing who to contact in an emergency and finding and accessing their crucial documents will not be an issue. Because this access is so important, we offer clients membership in our unique Lifetime Protection Program which helps them ensure their documents will be up to date and always available when needed, 24/7, anywhere in the world.

# EPILOGUE

## THE JOURNEY CONTINUES

## I. Recent Legislation and What It Means for Seniors and Boomers

On January 1, 2013, the Senate passed a compromise bill, called the American Taxpayer Relief Act of 2012 (ATRA), to avert the fiscal cliff; it passed overwhelmingly by a vote of eighty-nine to eight.

The ATRA is generally classified as tax legislation, but it has numerous provisions built into it that affect public benefits, elder care, and Elder Law.

What does this all mean for seniors and boomers? Consider the following:

1. Tax Rate Changes

   The bill permanently extended current tax rates for individuals earning less than $400,000 and couples earning less than $450,000. Wealthy taxpayers (individuals or couples making more than these amounts) will revert back to a 39.6 percent (up from 35 percent) tax rate. Taxpayers in this wealthy category will also see an increase in their capital gains tax rate and dividend tax rate from 15 percent to 20 percent. Also, married couples earning more than $300,000 and individuals that earn more than $250,000 will face a phaseout of the personal tax exemption.

2. Estate Tax Changes

   The estate tax is alive and well. The federal gift and estate tax exemption for 2013 will be $5.25 million per person and be indexed for inflation in future years. Effective January 1,

2013, the top federal estate tax rate will increase from 35 percent to 40 percent. Portability of the unused exemption will remain in place for spouses for federal taxes, but it is not recognized in Massachusetts and many other states. It is important to note, however, that since there is no portability in Massachusetts, a married couple must establish and maintain a tax effective estate plan if saving on estate taxes is one of the couple's goals and objectives. It is possible, with the right documents and coordination of savings and investments, for a married couple to pass a total of $2 million tax free. The Massachusetts estate tax exemption will remain at $1 million per person for 2013.

3. Payroll Tax

Since 2011, the payroll tax rate, which funds social security, was kept at 4.2 percent. Starting January 1, 2013, the payroll tax rate will revert back to 6.2 percent for those earning wages.

4. Good news for Physicians (and all of us)

For another year, doctors will not suffer the previously scheduled 27 percent reimbursement cuts to Medicare patients' fees.

5. Older Americans Act Funding

There is additional increased funding for important aging programs. For fiscal year 2013, area agencies on aging will receive $7.5 million in additional funds. The Aging and Disability Resource Centers received an additional $5 million. The National Center for Benefits and Outreach Enrollment will also see an increase of $5 million in funding. Also, Medicare State Health Insurance Programs (SHIP) will receive an additional $7.5 million in additional funding for 2013.

6. Sequestration

The scheduled automatic spending cuts are delayed by a few months. Half of the cuts would come from defense spending and the other half would come from nondefense spending. One area where spending cuts seem likely is Medicare and Medicaid benefits. We have already seen proposed legislation aimed at reducing government spending on these programs (see below for more details).

7. Class Act is Repealed

The CLASS Act was to be an attempt at a national long-term care insurance program. It was eliminated in exchange for the establishment of the Commission on Long-Term Care.

8. Commission on Long-Term Care

This commission will develop a plan for the establishment, implementation, and financing of a comprehensive system that ensures availability of long-term services and support. The commission will look into the coordination of Medicare, Medicaid, and private long-term care insurance. The commission will have fifteen members, including the president. The various members will represent the interests of consumers, older adults, family caregivers, healthcare workers, private long-term care insurance, state insurance departments, and state Medicaid agencies.

Let's hope Congress and the Commission on Long-Term Care come up with an effective, affordable long-term care model for boomers and seniors. In addition to hoping, people should be preparing for the future by taking responsibility for protecting their home and life savings, as well as being informed about health and financial topics that are a concern for many of the people we help.

Remember, the most painful financial crisis affecting seniors and boomers today is the devastating cost of long-term care ($12,000 to $15,000 per month, per person in the Greater Boston area!).

9. Other items

The bill extended Medicare programs for older Americans, including the payment for outpatient therapy services and specialized Medicare advantage plans for special needs individuals.

## II. What to Do Now?

This is complicated legislation, but don't let it stop you! Stay involved and informed. In addition to the information in this book, we will be monitoring the continuing changes in the months and years ahead. As information unfolds, we will provide guidance and insight through our blog, newsletters, and free reports. This continuing education and advice will help you be informed about these and future changes and how they may impact you and your family.

What should you be taking away from all the information in the *Senior & Boomers' Guide to Health Care Reform and Avoiding Nursing Home Poverty*? It is vital to review and improve your estate and asset protection planning now. It is critical to lock in the protection that is possible under the current laws before any changes that are being considered take effect. There have recently been two proposals before Congress that, though they have not passed, are very important to keep in mind.

### New Laws Proposed

### *Three-Year Veteran's Benefits Look-Back*

The first set of proposed changes introduced a three-year look-back period for Veteran's Benefits. The proposal, had it passed, would prevent a veteran from obtaining as much as $24,652 per year in valuable benefits. If a plan is implemented before a look-back period is passed, **veterans would not face a three-year waiting period**. They could qualify instantly. The delay could cost a veteran and their family nearly $75,000 of tax fee Veteran's Benefits if they had to wait out the three-year look-back period. Act now because this proposal may pass the next time it is introduced.

64

*Ten-Year Look-Back*

The other troublesome proposal that was introduced in 2012 was HR8300. This proposed legislation fortunately did not pass; however, the Congressional Budget Office (CBO) continues to study an increase of the current look-back period for Medicaid from five years to ten years. In 2006, during the Bush Era, when the look-back period was increased from three to five years for all transfers, the CBO projected $30 billion would be saved on seniors' Medicaid budget expenditures. The CBO is also reviewing a reduction in the home equity exemption for Medicaid purposes. Currently, in Massachusetts, a home is excluded as a countable asset (reviewed in detail earlier in this book) for values up to $802,000 for a married couple. The CBO is also reviewing legislation that would drop that exclusion to only $50,000; if passed, the equity in a home over $50,000 will not be an exempt asset. This will be a problem, especially for married couples who have not acted to protect themselves.

Unfortunately because of the state of the budget and the economy, those in Washington are still searching for mechanisms to balance the budget. The ATRA is now the law and will affect all citizens. What is of concern to many of our current and future clients is what is going to happen with health insurance and the Affordable Care Act and how it is going to produce the $716 billion in Medicare savings. Similarly, the Commission on Long-Term Care will also be reviewing (and possibly reducing) seniors' benefits for Medicare and Medicaid and the coordination benefits currently available to seniors, as well as how the services are made available in the various states. What this all means is that we cannot assume the status quo will continue because of increasing demand due to the growing number of seniors who need and qualify for care. At the same time there are increasing state and federal budget concerns.

## III. The Need to Be Proactive in Protecting Your Life Savings and Getting Quality Care

As we move forward as individuals and as a country, two things are clear: First, we need to vastly improve the quality of care delivered by our health system; and secondly, we all need to take greater responsibility in planning for long-term care and protecting our life savings from increasing medical and nursing home expenses.

To put things bluntly, our health-care system is failing seniors. The system is fragmented, confusing, and inefficient. People and their families are not able to figure out what to do, who to turn to, and what care to get for their loved one. People are confused and frustrated. In our current system, when seniors get sick or injured and are taken to the hospital, they are treated and cared for while in the hospital and then released with a complex set of instructions that would be difficult for anyone to follow, even a medical professional. In addition, they are given prescriptions, often more than one, and are left to take care of themselves with no follow-up or check-in from the care provider. See "The Problem" at Illustration A. All too often, the seniors end up taking medications incorrectly or failing to follow the complex instructions they were given; their condition worsens until once again they end up in the hospital, only to be discharged with another confusing set of instructions and multiple medications. This "Crisis Care" cycle is not working and is costing seniors a lot of money. See Illustration A for an illustration of the problem from the prospective of the patient receiving care. The problem can also be viewed from the perspective of the health-care provider. This illustration is from research developed in connection with new federal policy initiatives to increase health literacy to help the nation move beyond the cycle of costly "Crisis Care". For more information see *Health Affairs*, February 2012.

# The Problem

## The Problem, from the perspective of the patient/care receiver:

How do I manage my illness and not be a burden to my family?

## The Problem, from the perspective of the health care provider:[1]

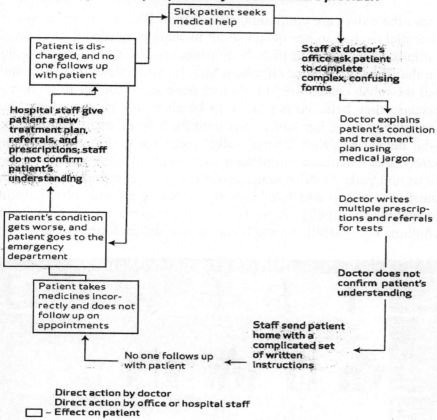

**Sick patient seeks medical help**

**Patient is discharged, and no one follows up with patient**

**Staff at doctor's office ask patient to complete complex, confusing forms**

**Hospital staff give patient a new treatment plan, referrals, and prescriptions; staff do not confirm patient's understanding**

**Doctor explains patient's condition and treatment plan using medical jargon**

**Doctor writes multiple prescriptions and referrals for tests**

**Patient's condition gets worse, and patient goes to the emergency department**

**Doctor does not confirm patient's understanding**

**Patient takes medicines incorrectly and does not follow up on appointments**

**No one follows up with patient**

**Staff send patient home with a complicated set of written instructions**

Direct action by doctor
Direct action by office or hospital staff
☐ – Effect on patient

### The Problem – Illustration A

When viewed from the perspective of the problem at Illustration A, you can develop an understanding and appreciate the importance of the need to not only increase your health literacy but also to have the tools to understand what you can do to not only stay healthy but also to protect yourself and your family as you evaluate, understand, and implement plans and ongoing resources for a protected future. Those who do take steps to plan for the elder care journey and develop a team of family and caring, dedicated professionals will be prepared

67

for the inevitable change in finances, health, and personal circumstances that arise.

## IV. Navigating the Elder Care Continuum

From the elder care continuum (Illustration B), we can see how the potential decline in health can result in changes needed in the home. Initially changes could include adjustments like adding a bathroom on the first floor. In one situation, Mrs. H. found that after a slip and fall the rehab center would not grant permission for her to go home because they believed her home to be an unsafe environment. She was able to make her home safer with the help of a care coordinator who helped her with a home safety assessment. Among the home safety check items recommended were to place no-slip strips on the floor and pads on the countertops, to remove extension cords from the floor, and to add handrails in the bathroom and other helpful locations. Eventually, Mrs. H. was allowed to return home and continue her rehabilitation at home, where she preferred to be.

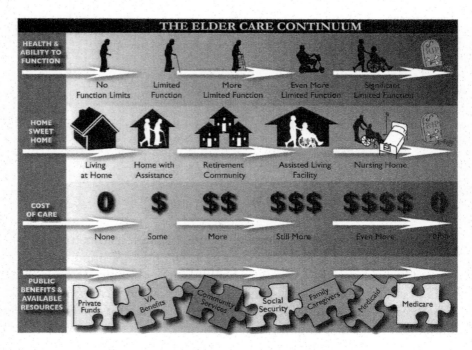

**The Elder Care Continuum – Illustration B**

Also illustrated on the elder care continuum (Illustration B) is the possibility of in-home care, which can be far less expensive than a nursing home. For some people in Massachusetts, we are able to locate in-home care resources that will help keep a senior at home as long as safely possible. The availability of community care resources and benefits, however, vary from state to state, depending on which policies are being followed. Medicaid paying for a nursing home has been recognized as the standard for caregiving when people can no longer take care of themselves, but most people, given a choice, would prefer to be at home or in the community and not in a nursing home.

The public benefit and available resources are represented in the bottom line on the elder care continuum. Until recently Medicare has denied payments for those with Alzheimer's, Parkinson's, or other illnesses for which there was no cure or possibility of improvement. Recent case law has changed this policy. As a result Medicare will pay for up to one hundred days of care for people who require skilled nursing and therapy to maintain their condition or slow deterioration, with care being provided in a nursing home, home, or outpatient therapy program.

As a result, Medicare may no longer deny a claim for benefits because the person cannot recover or get better. This is good news, although Medicare still pays for "up to one hundred days" in a rehabilitation facility or nursing home, but only if the person has first been in a hospital for at least three midnights as an inpatient rather than for observation. This categorization of 'inpatient' is critical as it affects both co-pay responsibility and access to Medicare to pay for rehab for up to one hundred days. This requirement of having spent three midnights in a hospital prior to Medicare paying for skilled care is an important and often overlooked part of the law. Currently, there is a bill pending in Congress to change the requirement that three midnights be spent in a hospital as an inpatient. This change would allow Medicare to cover one hundred days of care for patients admitted to the hospital for observation, who spent three midnights in the hospital. We will monitor the status of this change and provide information as new developments arise.

Each person and family is unique. The Elder Care Continuum (Illustration B) provides a model to reflect on while planning for the road ahead. As you can see from our description of the Elder Care Continuum, there are more changes coming. As discussed previously, the CBO is reviewing the impact of extending the look-back period from five to ten years and the U.S. Department of Veterans Affairs is reviewing the impact of adding a three-year look-back to qualify for veteran's benefits. Additionally, the Affordable Care Act has mandated $716 billion in Medicare savings to be identified, and we have a new fifteen person Committee on Long Term Care who will be studying Medicare, Medicaid, and long-term care, looking for opportunities to make changes in public benefits and affordable care resources along the elder care continuum. Many will find that they have peace of mind when they take responsibility for protecting themselves and their family. Those who do not plan ahead will be surprised at every turn by laws, policies, and inefficiencies in our health-care system, as well as rehabilitation and nursing home costs, as they are forced to spend their entire life savings at $12,000 to $15,000 per month. That's $144,000 to $180,000 per year. One of the many reasons to plan ahead and protect yourself and your family is that preparedness allows for more options and flexibility when the need for skilled care arises. Fortunately in Massachusetts there are several community resources available, so even for those who do not plan well in advance, there is access to alternative care. For more information on community resources and what you can do to protect yourself in advance or in emergency situations, please take a look at chapters 9 and 11 or visit www.DSullivan.com.

## V. The Hidden Cost of Caring for a Loved One

The difficulties of trying to get quality care for a loved one runs even deeper for those who are charged with providing the care themselves. In the past, a senior who needed full-time care could stay with family because most homes were one income homes, with one spouse available to care for an aging loved one. In today's world, a vast majority of families require income from both spouses, leaving no one at home to provide care. Those families who are able to provide care often experience what is called the 'Caregiver Strain'. See the Modified Caregiver Index – Illustration C. Caregiver Strain occurs as a result of being overloaded, trying to take care of your own work and family responsibilities while caring for a loved one. Many caregivers experience negative consequences, such as disturbed sleep, physical exhaustion or strain, emotional strain, feeling completely overwhelmed, and concern over how they will manage all their responsibility. In addition, caregivers are forced to change work plans, social plans, and family plans to meet the never ending demands of caring for an aging loved one.

You may ask yourself the following questions as you complete the form below. As you fill out the form, place a check mark in the column that applies to you. Your situation may be slightly different, but the item may still apply. This tool will be helpful for you to see if you will be benefitted by a more in-depth follow-up from an experienced care coordinator. We encourage you to contact a professional for more help.

Here is a list of things other caregivers have found to be difficult.

| | Yes, on a regular basis | Yes, sometimes | No |
|---|---|---|---|
| My sleep is disturbed | | | |
| Caregiving is inconvenient | | | |
| Caregiving is a physical strain | | | |
| Caregiving is confining | | | |
| There have been family adjustment | | | |
| There have been changes in personal plans | | | |
| There have been other demands on my time | | | |
| There have been emotional adjustments | | | |
| Some behavior is upsetting | | | |
| It is upsetting to find the person I care for has changed so much from his/her former self | | | |
| There have been work adjustments | | | |
| Caregiving is a financial strain | | | |
| I feel completely overwhelmed | | | |
| I wonder how I will manage | | | |
| I worry about the person I care for | | | |

Modified caregiver Strain Index; Hartford Institute of Geriatric Nursing, New York University.

**Modified Caregiver Strain Index – Illustration C**

# VI. Massachusetts as a Model for Community Care

We are fortunate to live in Massachusetts because of the great community-based care options and resources available to those who qualify. We have found that nearly everyone would prefer to be cared for at home or in the community, as opposed to a nursing home. There are a number of programs that are designed to deliver quality care to seniors at home, keeping them out of a nursing home or assisted living facility. It is simply a fact that those who stay in their home longer are happier and are frequently spending less on medical care when compared to those in an assisted living facility, paying $6,000 to $8,000 per month, or those in a nursing home, paying $12,000 to $15,000 per month. The Chronic Care Model at Illustration D represents a systems approach to improving chronic illness care which has been very effective for a number of families we serve.

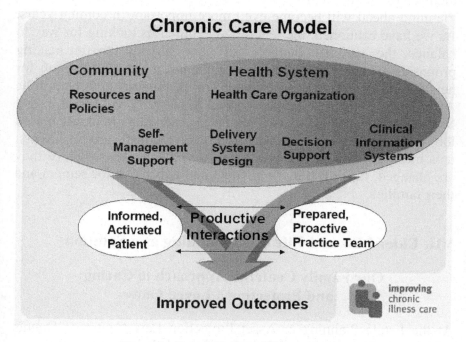

**Chronic Care Model – Illustration D**

We have seen improved health and well-being for clients and their families as a result of their participation in these community based programs. For more information on the community resources available to help keep you (or an aging loved one) in your home longer, please see www.DSullivan.com.

The cost of medical and long-term care is so great, it is critical that people and families take responsibility to be better informed about their options and potential improvements for their own care. It is also vital to plan ahead to protect their hard earned life savings, otherwise it will be required to be spent on your health care if you or your spouse need nursing home care. As you have read, in the Greater Boston Area, one month is a nursing home costs $12,000 to

$15,000 per month. If we extend that over a period of one year, you could end up paying $144,000 to $180,000 per year.

Those who plan ahead can protect their spouses, homes, and life savings. By facing reality and planning ahead, people are able to get themselves great quality care without going broke paying for it. Planning ahead will become even more important in coming years. As we have cautioned, the federal government is looking for way to balance the national budget and have already begun making proposals to increase look-back periods and make qualification for health-care benefits more difficult for seniors. Additionally, the Affordable Care Act aims to save $716 billion Medicare and Medicaid by reducing waste and over spending. With increased look-back periods and reduced spending on medical care for seniors, it is more important than ever to utilize existing laws, before they are changed, making it more difficult and expensive for seniors and their families.

## VII. Elder Law and Life Care Planning as a Solution

### Our Family Centered Approach to Caring and Protecting a Loved One

At the Estate Planning & Asset Protection Law Center of Dennis Sullivan & Associates, we help people and their families not only protect their hard-earned life savings but plan for incapacity and for possible long-term care needs, including home and community care, and the possibility of nursing home care. Our team of professionals will help locate and coordinate the best possible care, using either public or private resources to finance the cost of care. We do this through our unique Life Care Plan. A Life Care Plan is a client-centered, holistic approach to getting the client the care they need and getting the best possible result from medical care and treatment. Rather than focus solely on restructuring assets, we work to customize a long-term plan that serves as a road map to help people meet the inevitable challenges that come with aging.

People are guided by our Care Coordinator, who provides a Health Care Assessment during which she meets with people in their homes to assess their current care needs and project future needs. The purpose of the assessment is to accurately assess the individual's psychological, functional, and physical abilities in order to collaborate with the family to design a plan for current and future care and support needs. The Health Care Assessment will also evaluate the safety of the individual's home and the feasibility of the individual staying at home, as well as what family and other support is available.

Once we have an idea of the type and amount of care that will be needed, we are able to review, research and evaluate all options, and put the individual on course to receive the best possible care for their unique situation. Unlike the broken Crisis Care model discussed previously, our Care Coordinator works with the client and their family to provide ongoing monitoring and assessments. Our primary goal is to promote the good health, safety, and well-being of our clients, whether they are in a home environment, assisted living, or another setting.

The Chronic Care model draws on the best from research and practice, and it provides a foundation for collaborative programs, tools, and research aimed at improving care for the chronically ill. Studies show that a collaborative approach to managing chronic disease works. The Chronic Care model is based on the coordination of care to enable the patient to make seamless transitions from specialist to specialist to achieve the highest quality overall care. Care coordination is "the deliberate organization of patient care activities between two or more participants involved in a patient's care to facilitate the appropriate delivery of health-care services." [1] In this definition, all providers working with a particular patient share important clinical information and have clear, shared expectations about their roles. Equally important, they work together to keep patients and their families informed and to ensure that effective referrals and transitions take place.

[1] McDonald, K. M., Sundaram, V., Bravata, D. M., et al. *Closing the Quality Gap: A Critical Analysis of Quality Improvement Strategies, Volume 7—Care Coordination.* Rockville, MD: Agency for Healthcare Research and Quality, U.S. Department of Health and Human Services, June 2007.

## VIII. Final Thoughts

The medical system in this country is broken. Seniors get released from hospitals with confusing instructions and medications, and they consistently end up back in the hospital. This continuing cycle of Crisis Care is simply not working efficiently for seniors and their families. People are not getting the care they deserve and are being forced to spend their hard-earned life savings to pay for ineffective care. The system is confusing and difficult to navigate for seniors and their families. The cost of long-term care is on the rise and the government, faced with increasing deficits, has already proposed legislation to increase look-back periods and reduce spending on Medicare and Medicaid by $716 billion. Facing these realities, taking responsibility and planning ahead for potential long-term care is more important than ever.

Our unique role as Elder Law and Life Care Planning professionals enables our team to help you and your family navigate the difficult and confusing health-care system, to protect your life savings, and to remain at home or in the community for as long as it is safe, while you continue to receive the best care possible.

On behalf of the team of professionals at the Estate Planning & Asset Protection Law Center, I would like to thank you for reading our book. We hope you found it informative and helpful.

Sincerely,

The Team of Professionals at the Estate Planning & Asset Protection Law Center of Dennis Sullivan & Associates

CPSIA information can be obtained at www.ICGtesting.com
Printed in the USA
BVOW06s1505150715

408613BV00005BA/80/P